CROSSING the BORDER

CROSSING the BORDER

A community negotiates the transition
from early childhood to primary school

CAROL HARTLEY, PAT ROGERS, JEMMA SMITH,
SALLY PETERS, MARGARET CARR

NZCER PRESS

2012

NZCER Press
New Zealand Council for Educational Research
PO Box 3237
Wellington

© Carol Hartley, Pat Rogers, Jemma Smith, Sally Peters, Margaret Carr

ISBN 978-1-927151-47-1

All rights reserved

Designed by Lynn Peck, Central Media
Printed by Pinnacle Print, Wellington
Cover artwork by Angeline Vlasich

This title is also available as an e-book from www.nzcer.org.nz/nzcerpress

Distributed by NZCER
PO Box 3237
Wellington
New Zealand
www.nzcer.org.nz

CONTENTS

Foreword vii

Acknowledgements xi

CHAPTER 1 Border crossing and borderlands: The transition to school 1
    Transition to school in New Zealand 2
    An ecological approach to thinking about transitions 5
    How this book took shape 6
    How the book is organised 7

CHAPTER 2 Introducing the Mangere Bridge Project 9
    The communities 9
    The schools 11
    The transition-to-school project 12
    The research project 14

CHAPTER 3 Portfolios as tools for enhancing learning across the borders 17
    Portfolios at Mangere Bridge Kindergarten 18
    Transitioning with portfolios 21
    Portfolios go to school 22
    Concluding comments 27

CHAPTER 4 Mutually interesting projects 29
    A transition to school photo display board at the kindergarten 30
    The 'Welcome to School' DVD project 31
    Early childhood and primary links group 34
    Concluding comments 35

CHAPTER 5 Mutually familiar language, routines and practices 37
    School visits 38
    Playground book 41
    Information pamphlets and parent packs 41
    The school phonics DVD 43
    Waste free/zero rubbish 45
    Concluding comments 46

CHAPTER 6 The buddies project 47
    Tuakana/teina relationships 49
    The buddies project begins 50
    An ongoing project 52
    Concluding comments 55

CHAPTER 7 Theory building 57
    Retrospective data analysis and theorising 59
    Reciprocal relationships across sectors 63
    Concluding comments 65

CHAPTER 8 Multi-literacies that support the crossing of borders 67
    Multi-literacies 67
    Moviemaking 68
    Portfolios as multi-faceted documentation of learning 73
    Concluding comments 73

CHAPTER 9 Building bridges: The alignment between an early childhood
and a school curriculum 75
    A child's portfolio 77
    Key competency one: thinking (exploration) 79
    Key competency two: using language, symbols and texts (communication) 80
    Key competency three: managing self (well-being) 82
    Key competency four: relating to others (contribution) 84
    Key competency five: participating and contributing 86
    Concluding comments 87

CHAPTER 10 Conclusion 89
    Good will and professional relationships between teachers in action 90
    Fostering belonging and engagement in the new place 91
    Recognising the continuity of learning journeys 91

References 93

FOREWORD

Crossing the border—different countries, different landscapes, searching for the familiar, recognising the new, needing a map or a guide, bringing something with you, saying goodbyes, being met, shared journeys, changes and transitions, preparing for the journey, arriving at your destination, knowing you've got there. Transitions are a way of life for children today—as school start approaches many children are already veterans with a range of experience of out-of-home care and education. What is less known is how children navigate such change and how the adults in their lives can help to make transitions positive for them. The shared authorship of this book is informed by an exceptional teaching-research partnership that creates new insights into young children's experiences, the skills that early educators bring into play, and the contribution researchers can make to the process of transition.

Approaches to early childhood practices in New Zealand have excited policy makers, practitioners and researchers across the world since the original publication of *Te Whāriki* (Ministry of Education) in 1996. At the same time in my home country of Scotland we too were consulting on our first attempt at an early years curriculum framework which was published early the following year (SOEID, 1997). Questions about how early childhood practices link with and support children into the next stage of education are an inevitable outcome of defining curriculum for the youngest children. Over the years policy frameworks have brought an increasing focus on linking ECE and school, but whether the two sectors are structurally tightly or loosely coupled, or the curriculum is distinctive or aligned, there is a need to consider how such educational journeys affect children's wellbeing and learning both immediately and in the longer term.

Here is a book that brings together different forms of knowledge and experience and focuses on the local. Consequently the importance of understanding young children's experience in context is emphasized and the inter-personal and socio-cultural nature (Dunlop, 2010) of early childhood transitions is recognized. The ten chapters take the reader through the complex process that is transition, by addressing the need for mutual views, building connections, addressing difference, sharing approaches of mutual interest (such as the use of portfolios), a buddy scheme and movie making and underpinning the practical day-to-day by theory building and new alignments between early childhood and school; between Mangere Bridge Kindergarten and two of its partner schools, their families and communities.

Mangere Bridge Kindergarten became a Centre of Innovation focusing on transitions. As a result of their years of collaboration the team of teacher-researchers and university-researchers—Carol Hartley, Pat Rogers, Jemma Smith, Sally Peters and Margaret Carr—provide a serious, delightful and accessible read that at the same time challenges new thinking and invites well-thought through and innovative practice.

Three interpretations of crossing borders are central in their research process: crossing borders between kindergarten and school; crossing borders across languages and literacies; crossing borders between *Te Whāriki* and the school curriculum.

Shared expectations amongst teachers in early childhood and school settings, curriculum linking, coming together for further shared learning, working collaboratively with families and listening to and being informed by children are central to this book and to transition processes. As readers we are privileged to take part in the work done by Mangere Bridge Kindergarten and to benefit from the thinking—the working theories—of the teaching team.

As good practice is shared, so too must be the message that one way does not suit all, and that a variety of well thought through approaches may be needed in order to support different children in ways that work for them. My experience of transitions research, policy and practices tells me that continuity matters a lot for some children, difference and change is needed for others, and a further group really need to be able to make a fresh start at times of transition (Dunlop, 2010). I am struck by how young children might help each other and how to elicit their advice—so that children's funds of knowledge around transitions build and become a source of confidence and wellbeing to meet the new and to reflect on important connections such as those exemplified as a 'Cross Sector Pathway' in Chapter 9 of this book.

Will structural borders continue to influence children's school entry? Almost inevitably! The separation of early childhood and school, the ways in which we construct education and sustain the separateness of ECE through a distinctive philosophy (Lenz Taguchi, 2010), separate curriculum, different sectoral based training for practitioners, and the different expectations of each new phase of education mean that continued attention is needed to border crossing transitions. The continuous process of transition to school in New Zealand affects both sectors and all of the adults and children involved on an almost daily basis as birthdays come round and new 5-year-olds step off from their early childhood setting into school. For the sake of all children there is a need to make transitions partnerships that continue to address continuity, the linking of curriculum, the alignment of learning dispositions and key competences and to ensure that educators each side of this boundary are well informed about each other's practices and culture and recognize their shared community, whilst taking account of the individual child and their family.

Children, families, early childhood and school teachers, communities, communities of practice and research communities are all visible in *Crossing the border*—it is a wonderful and stimulating read and it makes the strongest case possible for collaboration so that real understanding can be developed about what transitions mean for children and in turn what that means for family and professional practices. I thank all the authors for the opportunity to take part in their world and look forward to return trips to New Zealand in coming years.

Emeritus Professor Aline-Wendy Dunlop
University of Strathclyde, Scotland

References

Dunlop, A-W. (October, 2010). *The theoretical foundations and some key results of transitions to school research in a Scottish context: one framework or many? Populating the theoretical model over time.* Starting School Research, Policy and Practice Event, Charles Sturt University, Albury, Australia.

Lenz Taguchi, H. (2010). *Going Beyond the Theory/Practice Divide in Early Childhood Education: Introducing an intra-active pedagogy.* London and New York: Routledge.

Ministry of Education. (1996). *Te whāriki. He whāriki mātauranga mō ngā mokopuna o Aotearoa: Early childhood curriculum.* Wellington: Learning Media.

SOEID (1997). *A Curriculum Framework for Children in their Pre-school Year.* Edinburgh: Scottish Office Education and Industry Department.

CROSSING the BORDER

ACKNOWLEDGEMENTS

The Centre of Innovation project outlined in this book took place over three years and the resultant research ethos and testing of innovative ideas has become part of the culture of Mangere Bridge Kindergarten. Initially the inspiration was to create an environment for successful transitions for our children and families and the more we learnt the more possibilities we could see. We built our research on earlier learning from work with the *Strengthening Education In Mangere and Otara Project* (SEMO) and with Educational Leadership Project (Ltd) and are indebted to Wendy Lee for her dedication to research in early childhood education. We are also grateful to Sue Dockett and Bob Perry for their inspiring work around transition to school in Australia.

The teaching team Carol, Pat and Jemma would like to **say a huge thank you** to the Centre of Innovation (COI) programme which gave us the opportunity to research in depth our innovations around transition to school and to work so closely with Margaret and Sally, co-authors of this book. We have grown enormously as researchers and academics nurtured by their outstanding support. We also appreciate the friendship and collegial support of the centres of Round Three COI; Botany Downs kindergarten (especially Bronwyn, conference buddy and critical friend), Greerton Early Childhood centres, Wadestown Kindergarten and Bush Street Kindergarten, Rangiora who became our Hui buddies; and in particular Anne Meade for her dedication to children's learning. Roskill South Kindergarten (Round one, COI) led the way for us and we are extremely grateful to Karen for supporting us in our application and on our journey.

Transition in all its forms continues to have a life of its own at Mangere Bridge Kindergarten. The research has continued well beyond the initial COI project and the teaching team has recently initiated a relationship with another school, across the bridge, extending our transition relationships outside of our own community.

The school buddies have a special place in our acknowledgements as without their friendships with the kindergarten children one whole chapter would not have been possible.

Our long journey has sometimes taken our attention away from home and we would like to thank all of our families for being so supportive over this time.

Also the teaching team would like to thank the Auckland Kindergarten Association for their support; past teaching team members Kathy, Frances and Sarah; Alexandra and then Avis who so ably replaced us whenever we needed a reliever; Ann Hatherly from CORE Education; Nola Harvey from the University of Auckland for support in dissemination and the Faculty of Education Research Committee at the University of Waikato for overseeing ethical approvals. Our original administrator, Stephanie, was so enthusiastic about the idea of this journey, and our current administrator, Ingrid, continues this tradition; thank you both.

All the authors believe the strategies, philosophies, and pedagogies contained within this book are not only limited or relevant to a single transition from early childhood to primary but rather can be applied to transitions throughout education. Within the research we identified the importance and interconnectedness of relationships: relationships with the children and families, with the schools, with the local community and into the wider education community.

This book is the result of those relationships. We are all indebted to the children and families of the Mangere Bridge community who trusted us and have **unstintingly** contributed their enthusiasm and commitment to the project. We wish to acknowledge all those who have contributed time, energy, enthusiasm and feedback to the research, especially the teachers and community of the local schools, Mangere Bridge School and Waterlea Primary School. Warm thanks go, too, to Aline-Wendy for her contribution in writing the foreword.

Carol, Pat and Jemma
Mangere Bridge Kindergarten

CHAPTER 1

Border crossing and borderlands: The transition to school

Starting school is one of the many transitions that children in modern societies experience. Brooker (2008) notes that "everyone who works with children has witnessed the impact that these transitions can have on their learning, essentially through an impact on their well-being" (p. 1). This book documents and discusses a number of innovations that were developed to build relationships and to support children's learning across the borders between home, early childhood education and school. Although the main focus of the book is the transition to school, many of the ideas discussed can be applied to other transitions.

In our approach to starting school we have adopted Fabian and Dunlop's (2002) definition of transition as a holistic, dynamic experience that takes place over an extended period:

> The word transition is referred to as the process of change that is experienced when children (and their families) move from one setting to another ... It includes the length of time it takes to make such a change, spanning the time between any pre-entry visit(s) and settling-in, to when the child is more fully established as a member of the new setting. (p. 3)

In fact it is our belief that the process begins even earlier, when the first thoughts about making that move occur. Then, as children move from an early childhood setting into school, this involves crossing both a physical and a cultural 'border'. There is both a symbolic as well as a literal change of environments. It is a time of change for children and their families, and as such it offers up many opportunities, but also dilemmas and challenges that must be faced. We have focused on the notion of border crossing because, as Peters (2004) discussed, it does not imply that transitions will be difficult, but neither does it avoid the fact that some are.

On either side of the border to be crossed are the early childhood and school sectors, which can each be thought of as different cultures. Each culture "represents the shared values, traditions and belief characteristics of the setting" (Fabian & Dunlop, 2002, p. 2). Within each of these cultures teaching, learning and assessment may be different, and where this is the case, what it means to be a learner is constructed differently (Peters, 2004). Starting school is therefore a time when at least two cultures have to be negotiated. In making the transition between cultures the child moves into different realms of meaning, knowledge and social forms. However, these differences between settings are socially constructed. Britt and Sumsion (2003) explored an alternative possibility, that of shared "space" between early childhood and school, a borderland:

> We can now look for and work toward connections and intersections between two different places—points of negotiation, of cohabitation, meshing, transforming, combining. Whereas before, the focus was on the gap between early childhood education and primary education as a void, a site of non-existence (because within that model you are either one/or the other, never both, or between the two), now it is a valid space, a site of connection, intersection and overlap. The borderland is a space not only of existence, but of coexistence. (Britt & Sumsion, 2003, p. 133)

This book includes many examples of early childhood and school teachers working together to help children to navigate the borders they encounter, while also reducing the divide to create some shared spaces or borderlands.

Transition to school in New Zealand

It is not just the cultures of early childhood education and school that are socially constructed. The age at which children start school is also socially determined. Children in New Zealand, for whom schooling is not compulsory until age six, typically start school on their fifth birthday. This means New Zealand children are some of the youngest on school entry among Western countries. For example, Suggate (2009) notes that only 4 out of 56 OECD countries in a recent PISA (Programme for International Student Assessment) study had a school entry age under six.

The system of beginning school on one's fifth birthday makes transition to school in New Zealand a very individual event. It means that on any day of the week a child may be leaving an early childhood service and beginning school the next day. Early years transitions are therefore an ongoing process throughout the year, and consequently children often go into a new entrant class by themselves and may or may not know children in their new class. As a result, school teachers are faced with new children starting throughout the year, joining an ongoing programme, while in early childhood settings teachers farewell children throughout the year, while also transitioning new children in to take their place. This can create challenges for all concerned. However, although entering an established class as the only new person can sometimes mean children are faced with bewildering experiences during their first days (see, for example, Ledger, 2000; Peters, 2004), it is worth noting that overseas alternatives such as term intakes into an existing class can also be difficult for both groups (Fabian, 1998).

Curriculum documents help to shape ideas about learners and learning within each sector. In New Zealand, the early childhood curriculum, *Te Whāriki* (Ministry of Education, 1996), covers education from birth to school entry, while the school curriculum covers learning during the school years. In recent years there have been considerable changes to the school curriculum as schools moved from *The New Zealand Curriculum Framework* (Ministry of Education, 1993) to *The New Zealand Curriculum* (Ministry of Education, 2007). With regard to starting school, one of the important changes to the school curriculum was the introduction of "key competencies", which align with the strands of the early childhood curriculum, *Te Whāriki*. Key competencies are dispositional and draw on "knowledge, attitudes and values in ways that lead to action" (Ministry of Education, 2007, p. 12). They provide an opportunity for teachers in both the early childhood and school sectors to explore how the key competencies link to the learning dispositions in the early childhood curriculum, and how dispositions and competencies can be used and interpreted in complementary ways.

The current school curriculum also highlights the importance of transition experiences, and notes that the transition from early childhood education to school is supported when the school:

- fosters a child's relationship with teachers and other children and affirms their identity;
- builds on the learning experiences that the child brings with them;
- considers the child's whole experience of school;
- is welcoming of family and whānau.[1]

(Ministry of Education, 2007, p. 41)

In addition to the curriculum documents in each sector, various plans and strategies have drawn attention to the importance of the transition to school. Firstly, the Ministry of Education's (2002) 10-year strategic plan for early childhood included a goal of promoting collaborative relationships between early childhood education (ECE) services, families, other services and programmes and schools. The following actions were suggested to help achieve the proposed strategy of "promoting coherence of education between birth and eight years":

- promoting better understanding between ECE teachers and primary teachers about the links between *Te Whāriki* and *The New Zealand Curriculum Framework*

---
1 Whānau: The Māori term for extended family.

- promoting better understanding between ECE teachers and primary teachers about the pedagogical approaches in ECE and schools
- distributing information about effective transition from ECE to school practices.

(Ministry of Education, 2002, p. 17)

The Commissioner for Children's (2006) 10-year long-term vision for the wellbeing of children in New Zealand, *Te Ara Tukutuku ngā Whanaungatanga o ngā Tamariki*, also highlighted transitions as points of key interest. Assessment at key transition points—such as school entry—was recommended with a view to ensuring resources are available to manage the transition well (Commissioner for Children, 2006). Health initiatives such as B4 School checks, which started in 2008 (Ministry of Health, 2008), fit within the Commissioner for Children's proposal to have a plan for each child and to identify where additional support is required. In addition, improving transitions to school has been identified as a key goal in *Ka Hikitia—Managing for Success: The Māori[2] Education Strategy 2008–2012* (Ministry of Education, 2008a) and as a key factor in Pasifika[3] success in the *Pasifika Education Plan 2008–2012* (Ministry of Education, 2008b).

Following the publication of these strategies and plans, the Ministry of Education commissioned a literature review to examine the research evidence regarding successful transitions. The findings are presented in Peters (2010). Overall, the review concluded that successful transitions depend on:

> features of a school environment that foster children's well-being, belonging and positive engagement with learning. Responsive, reciprocal, relationships between all concerned is a key feature of a successful transition. Related to this, a successful transition will include teachers who affirm the child's identity and culture, connect with and build on the children's funds of knowledge from early childhood education and home, and hold positive expectations for success which includes seeing promise in new entrant learners rather than deficits. (p. 73)

Although the review highlighted the fact that there is still much to be learnt about the transition to school and the ways in which this can be enhanced, it did indicate the power of classroom practices and other contextual factors that shape children's experiences.

Interest in transitions in New Zealand reflects a trend in many other countries. For example, the Educational Transitions and Change (ETC) Research Group's (2011) position statement drew together researchers from around the world to work with educators and policy makers to clarify aspirations for all those involved in this aspect of children's lives. Ongoing work in this area is important because although the curriculum and the strategic plans in New Zealand signal a commitment to enhancing children's

---

2   Māori: indigenous person/people of Aotearoa New Zealand.
3   Pasifika: person/peoples of Pacific Island descent.

transition to school, and the Ministry's literature review highlights ways in which successful transitions can be supported, in practice there appears to be considerable variation in transition arrangements. Anecdotal evidence from a range of settings across the country suggests that during the time prior to starting school, when a parent/caregiver is expected to enrol a child, the arrangements for sharing information and for children and families to visit school can vary considerably. The degree of connection between early childhood services and schools also varies, and an added layer of complexity is the number of schools that children from one early childhood service may go to, along with the number of early childhood services feeding into any one school. As with other aspects of transition, there is no norm.

This book draws on the experiences of early childhood and school teachers who have been addressing these issues for a number of years and offers a range of strategies that can be adapted to other settings. It is co-authored by three of these experienced teachers.

An ecological approach to thinking about transitions

Bronfenbrenner's (1979) ecological theory provides a theoretical framework for considering innovative approaches to supporting the transitions discussed in this book. This framework is central to the early childhood curriculum, *Te Whāriki* (Ministry of Education, 1996, p. 19), and offers a valuable perspective on the complex interweaving of factors that help to shape children's transition journeys (Peters, 2004). Bronfenbrenner directs attention to the different levels of the environment (micro-, meso-, exo- and macrosystems) and how they both influence and are influenced by a developing person. The microsystems are the patterns of activities, roles and relationships experienced in a given setting. Starting school is an example of an ecological transition, which occurs "whenever a person's positioning in the ecological environment is altered as a result of change of role or setting, or both" (Bronfenbrenner, 1979, p. 26).

Earlier, Carr (1998) wrote of the "bi-mondial" 4-year-old, who spends time in the two worlds of home and early childhood service, becoming a tri-mondial child at 5 and figuring out the roles, rules and relationships in at least three worlds (home, early childhood service and school). Within this theoretical approach, transition can be understood in terms of the child taking on the role of the pupil. Hill, Comber, Louden and Rivalland (1998) argued that learning the culture of the school, and their role within it (i.e., what it means to "do school"), was a necessary step before children could focus on the *content* of schooling.

Returning to Bronfenbrenner, the mesosystem comprises the inter-relationships between the microsystems. Events in one microsystem can affect what happens in another (Bronfenbrenner, 1986). There may be connections between them (e.g., a child's siblings and friends may be present at both home and school), and communication between settings is also important. Smith

(1998) maintains that if there are "warm, reciprocal and balanced relationships between preschool and school teachers the transition will be supportive of development" (p. 14).

The exosystem refers to settings that do not involve the developing person but affect or are affected by what happens in the microsystem. Three exosystems that Bronfenbrenner (1986) saw as likely to be particularly influential in a child's development are the parents' workplace, the parents' social networks, and community influences on family functioning. Wider school processes, policies and beliefs also have an impact on what happens for children, and they are central to understanding individual transition experiences.

The macrosystem refers to the overriding beliefs, values, ideology, practices and so on that exist, or could exist, within a culture (Bronfenbrenner, 1979). Significant features of the macrosystem in New Zealand are the practice of children moving to school as they turn five, the strategic plans and strategies to improve transitions, and the early childhood and school curriculum documents that help to shape teacher practice in each setting.

The ideas discussed in each chapter of this book also draw on sociocultural theories and acknowledge the value of considering the social and cultural processes influencing children's learning (Wertsch & Tulviste, 1992). Children learning under adult guidance or in collaboration with more capable peers (Vygotsky, 1978, p. 86) is central to this view. Ideally, this collaboration is characterised by mutual understanding or intersubjectivity (Rogoff, 1990). This requires a context of shared meaning and understanding to be established, so that the person working with a learner can sensitively adjust the scaffolding to extend the learner's development. Children need to feel accepted and tuned in to teachers, and vice versa (Smith, 1998).

How this book took shape

This book is the most recent outcome of a history of action research in one early childhood centre, Mangere Bridge Kindergarten. Professional collaboration with teachers at one of the local schools and an interest in research began for Mangere Bridge Kindergarten in 1999 with the SEMO (Strengthening Education in Mangere and Otara) and ECPL (Early Childhood Primary Links) projects, which involved professional development with Stuart McNaughton and Gwenneth Phillips (Robinson, Timperley, & Bullard, 2000). That research fostered shared expectations among teachers in early childhood and school settings and illustrated the positive effects for children in the area of literacy achievement. It was reported in *Picking up the Pace* (Phillips, McNaughton, MacDonald, & Keith, 2002). This coming together for professional development became the starting point for the teachers' interest in transition to school issues and challenges, and illuminated a number of possibilities.

Further opportunities for reflective practice arose when the team at the kindergarten worked on other projects with the Educational Leadership Project. These projects had a focus on transition to school, and in 2004 specifically linked to assessment for learning practices using the *Kei Tua o te Pae* resource (Carr, Lee, Jones, 2004, 2007, 2009). The relationship with one of the local schools had moved beyond the kindergarten teachers visiting the school, to maintain the links built at the time of the SEMO project, to coming together to debate and discuss the nature of teaching and learning. This took the form of meetings to develop common ground in terms of understanding what counts as valued learning in each setting.

After nearly 7 years of research and collaboration with one local school, Mangere Bridge Kindergarten became a Centre of Innovation (2006–2008) with a focus on transition to school. Centres of Innovation were initiated by the Ministry of Education to promote research based on innovative practices already underway in early childhood centres and to disseminate the findings within the early childhood community. The aim of the Mangere Bridge Kindergarten Centre of Innovation project was to continue the discussion that arose out of the earlier research debates. This is described further in Chapter 2.

How the book is organised

Chapter 2 provides details of Mangere Bridge Kindergarten's Centre of Innovation project. The next seven chapters explore theories that help to understand and support transitions, illustrated with data from Mangere Bridge Kindergarten's research. Chapter 3 considers the role of portfolios in fostering children's learning journeys. Chapter 4 describes work to foster cross-sector relationships through a range of joint projects, the most successful of which were those that were mutually interesting to a range of participants.

Many of the projects described in Chapters 3 and 4 produced artifacts, and these in turn provided transitioning children with language, routines and common practices they could take across the border with them. Chapter 5 discusses these mutually familiar tasks and artifacts and the ways in which they can foster belonging for children and families and develop connections between contexts and curriculum documents. Chapter 6 discusses the role of school buddies and how they enhance transitions for the younger children. Chapter 7 introduces a framework for analysing what was important for the success of the projects discussed in Chapters 3 to 6.

Multi-literacies in use within the kindergarten context, and the role of these as "priming events", is the focus of Chapter 8, while Chapter 9 discusses the linked learning between learning dispositions and key competencies, with examples from the case study of one child. The overall conclusions in Chapter 10 provide some key messages for teachers working within their own contexts to enhance the experiences of children and families as they make the transition from early childhood education to school.

CROSSING the BORDER

CHAPTER 2

Introducing the Mangere Bridge Project

Many researchers have identified that a child's experience of transition into primary school is linked to children's emotional wellbeing, social competence and cognitive development, and they discuss the impact of a successful transition on ongoing educational outcomes and later life skills (Brostrom, 2005; Bulkeley & Fabian, 2006; Dockett & Perry, 2007; Early, Pianta, & Cox, 1999). The overarching rationale for the teachers and researchers in the project discussed in this book was to work towards a successful transition to school for the children. Giroux (1992) has described the desirability of creating conditions in which people can become border crossers who try to understand a new culture or setting in its own terms rather than applying their own cultural lenses to something new. Gaining insights into the 'other' or new culture can disrupt existing divides and open new possibilities. Seeking this understanding on many levels, rather than making judgments about the other setting based on their own early childhood or school culture, and trialing ways of supporting learners to make these border crossing transitions, were central to the work of the teachers in this setting.

The communities

Three communities were involved in this project: the Mangere Bridge community, the education community and the kindergarten community. Mangere Bridge is a suburb in South Auckland, New Zealand. Geographically, it is situated on a peninsula between the Manukau Harbour and Mangere mountain, surrounded by foreshore park and the regional park of Ambury Farm. This area was settled first by Māori and then by diverse groups of immigrants. Pākehā[4] built baches beside the sea in a holiday settlement. Later,

---

4 Pākehā: Māori term for New Zealander(s) of European descent.

Chinese families developed market gardens, and later again Pasifika people came here as part of the greater Mangere area development in the 1950s and 1960s. These earlier immigration waves were followed by immigrants from India, South-East Asia, Fiji and the African continent.

The waves of immigration have resulted in a community that is ethnically, culturally and economically diverse. The sea and the mountain are very significant in the lives of both local iwi[5] and the families of the community. The community is close knit, with some parents who grew up in Mangere Bridge now raising their own children here. Many families begin their community involvement with Plunket[6] play group and the puzzle library. Then they attend kindergarten or Playcentre,[7] and later become involved in community and sports organisations such as scouts, guides, soccer and baseball. The township is small but very active, with community events such as the Christmas Santa parade, the Ambury Farm Day, and music and food festivals.

The local education community comprises Mangere Bridge Kindergarten (established in 1975), a Playcentre, a private education and care centre, a Pasifika education and care centre at the local Catholic Church, and three primary schools. There is no intermediate or high school in the area, and local children cross Mangere Bridge each day (by bus or car) to attend Royal Oak Intermediate and Onehunga High School. Although there are three primary schools in the area, the majority of children from the kindergarten transition to one of two local schools, both of which are within walking distance of the kindergarten.

Mangere Bridge Kindergarten is a sessional early childhood education facility situated in a cul-de-sac within the residential community. The families at the

---

5 Iwi: confederation of related tribes.
6 Plunket: a national child health community organization for children under 5.
7 Playcentre: a national parent cooperative early childhood organisation.

kindergarten identify with approximately 15 different cultural backgrounds, and many identify with more than one culture. Shortly before the project began, a 2005 survey showed the demographic mix as approximately 40 percent Pākehā, 20 percent Māori, 15 percent Pasifika, and 10 percent Asian or South-East Asian, with the remainder made up of people from Middle Eastern, African, Australian and British ethnicities. By 2008 our ethnicity statistics showed some changes: 36 percent Pākehā, 27 percent Māori, 20 percent Pasifika, 10 percent Asian or South-East Asian, and 7 percent other, which includes Australian, South African, British, Czech and Spanish[8] people. The kindergarten has a strong and interested parent/whānau group, who work actively to provide resources, information and support. Many families are also actively involved as members of other local community organisations, even though both parents often work full or part time.

The schools

The two schools in this transition project are Mangere Bridge School and Waterlea Primary School. Both of these schools are in mixed socio-economic communities. It is perhaps best to let the schools describe themselves:

> Mangere Bridge School is over 100 years old. It has a multicultural mix of children, with equal numbers of Māori, NZ European and Pasifika students and a smaller number of Asian and Indian children. The school has always enjoyed huge support from the community, and many students at the school have parents and grandparents who attended this school. For many years the school has run a popular weekly *Wonderful Wednesday* programme for children under 5 years of age. It also hosts a weekly Gifted and Talented preschool programme called Small Poppies. The facilities are superb for learning, with a swimming pool and auditorium, as well as grounds referred to by the younger students as 'The Park'.
>
> Waterlea Primary School has a strong family atmosphere. The school culture is enhanced with everyone at Waterlea Primary School living by the Waterlea Primary School Way where we look after ourselves, we look after others, we look after our environment and we look after our learning. The school's Awhi[9] programme assesses the hauora[10] needs of the children. Using the results of the assessment, programmes are planned and implemented to ensure that children get all the help and support they require both in and out of the classroom. The school enjoys strong support from our parent and wider communities. Mums' and Dads' Day, a student initiative, is a popular event on our annual calendar. It is a chance for families to be hosted by their children, to enjoy learning something together and see what goes on in their child's school day. The school has a biennial gala where the whole school's community members pool their energy to raise funds and have fun together. Leadership is fostered at all levels of the school. This can be seen in student led activities such as the

---

8 Auckland Kindergarten Association (2005, 2008) Unpublished Statistics Data.
9 Awhi: to embrace or cherish.
10 Hauora: a Māori philosophy of health and well-being unique to New Zealand.

weekly assemblies and Cool Schools, a peer mediation programme. The school is committed to the use of smart tools to aid learning and so is gradually increasing the use of ICT equipment in all classrooms.

At the outset of this project the kindergarten team wished to develop and strengthen relationships with these two crucial partners in the transition process. Having two main schools to work with provided an opportunity to research deeply because of the bounded nature of our context. While we realise that this is not always the case for many early childhood education centres, who may have children going to a large number of schools, it did give us the opportunity to explore transition from a manageable perspective, especially when beginning to develop relationships in the community.

The transition-to-school project

At Mangere Bridge Kindergarten, as for many other early childhood centres, in any given week one child may leave for school, or it may be up to four or five children. As an example, during one 4-month period of this research project 30 children transitioned to school; overall, 259 children transitioned during the three-year project. This contributes to continually changing groups, interactions and relationships. It also has a high impact on workload for both early childhood and primary school teachers.

In thinking about transition for our children and families, we like to use this photo of a child jumping out of a tree as an analogy for the transition to school process. It is not an easy process to prepare to jump—in this case the crook of the tree is a difficult place to get your feet right—and then it is a leap into space before landing on the safety mat. We think the child initially

may be feeling apprehensive, worried about who is looking, who will be there as support, and what happens if it doesn't go as planned. However, this book is about the ways in which a kindergarten and the contributing schools have provided safe and satisfying landings.

Our philosophy statement places emphasis on the principles of *Te Whāriki*, particularly partnerships with children, teachers, families and the community. Transition partnerships are a valuable part of our work as early childhood teachers, and our involvement in several research projects (see Chapter 1) had highlighted for us the need to place extra emphasis on this important aspect of teaching in early childhood education. *Te Whāriki* addresses the need for links between the early childhood curriculum and the primary school curriculum, stating: that "The early childhood curriculum provides a foundation for children to become confident and competent and, during the school years to be able to build on their previous learning" (Ministry of Education, 1996, p. 93). Similarly, the school curriculum recognises the importance of building on children's earlier learning and shows the alignment between the strands of *Te Whāriki* and the key competencies in the school curriculum.

At the outset of the research we believed that the specific strength of our innovative approach to transition to school in this kindergarten was the collegial and collaborative relationship with the teaching team at one local school. The innovation was the result of the culture of research collaboration between the kindergarten teachers, the junior school teaching team and the principals and deputy principal. Carol Hartley, the head teacher at the kindergarten, had built a relationship with the principal and deputy principal that extended back over more than 10 years. This ongoing relationship has been instrumental in strengthening the relationship between the kindergarten team and the school. Building on this innovation by way of the research project matched our passion and enthusiasm for exploring transition and provided a degree of continuity and complexity in our dealings with the school teachers.

This relationship is a living example of the ways in which teachers from both sectors can work together to support coherence in education, one of the ideas of the 10-year strategic plan for early childhood education, noted earlier (Ministry of Education, 2002, p. 17). However, we were aware, from our own experience and from reading earlier research, that developing this level of understanding and fostering effective relationships between early childhood education and school is not always easy (Robinson, Timperley, & Bullard, 2000; Timperley, McNaughton, Howie & Robinson, 2003). For example, Timperley et al. (2003) found that "despite a commitment to collaborate, teachers from the two sectors (ECE and primary) had very different expectations of each other and most were dissatisfied with the current arrangements" (p. 32).

Dissatisfaction with existing arrangements was evident in our own experiences, too. As we developed the proposal for the Centre of Innovation project we surveyed all the parents of children in the kindergarten and those who had transitioned to school in the past two terms. A number of parents suggested that the kindergarten could do more transition work with local schools. With these views in mind we began to develop our research questions.

The research project

The research team and authors of this book

The authors of this book are the research team for the Mangere Bridge Kindergarten Centre of Innovation project. Carol, Pat and Jemma are the kindergarten teaching team. All three teachers hold early childhood degree qualifications and are registered. Two research associates, Margaret and Sally, were invited to work with the teacher-researchers, based on their knowledge of the field.

Research design

The nature of the data-gathering for the work discussed in this book afforded the opportunity to follow a strategy suggested by Mills (2000), which involved experiencing, enquiring into and examining the data as the project developed. It was an action research process, enabling unexpected directions. Change was factored into the research design to allow for flexibility and the spiralling nature of action research (Bell, 1999; Mills, 2000). This included evaluation while research was underway in order to ascertain the next step or spiral in the action research process (Aubrey, David, Godfrey, & Thompson, 2000). This approach is necessarily complex and recursive (Graue & Walsh, 1998), something that was evident as the research team (teacher-researchers and university-researchers) sought deeper meanings and understanding of the situation being studied.

Action research changes the traditional role of researcher, from being removed from the subject to working alongside and with the participants in the research; listening, observing and reflecting on the data to influence teacher practice (Cardno, 2003). Kagan and Neuman (1998) believe that action research may help to "bridge the research-to-practice gap that exists in the field of transition" (p. 373). Reporting on three decades of research on transition, Kagan and Neuman (1998) proposed a multi-pronged approach to research on transition to promote action research using multiple data collection methods and perspectives. Our study reflected this approach, drawing on multiple methods and a range of perspectives. Data collection and data sources included:

- observations in the kindergarten and the new entrant classrooms
- interviews with new entrant teachers, deputy principals and principals
- focus group interviews with 5- and 6-year-olds at the school
- semi-structured interviews with nearly-5-year-olds at kindergarten

- focus group interviews with parents of children from each school after the children had made the transition
- case studies that exemplify specific aspects of border crossing
- children's portfolios at the kindergarten
- teaching stories and teacher journals in the kindergarten (during the project, teachers wrote teaching stories to contribute to the planning for emergent interests and projects, and recorded their reflections in journals).

Throughout the project there was an intention to continue the emerging relationship with children, families and schools as research partners. Fasoli (2003) discusses seeing children as competent in helping to construct "the joint enterprise" in her research with young children (p.11). We actively listened to the views of children in a range of ways using discussions of photographs, documents and artifacts of various kinds, including their portfolios. Children also contributed by selecting examples of photos to be included in their portfolios, dictating stories, building transition books and commenting on valued learning dispositions and key competencies from their point of view.

Parents contributed family stories and feedback on the work. Together with the teachers at the two schools, we were keen to explore how these key competencies could link to the learning dispositions aim in the early childhood curriculum, and how dispositions and competencies could be used and interpreted in complementary ways.

Research questions

The research questions were framed around the analogy of crossing a border from one place to another, and one language to another, with the children's portfolios as a passport in the border crossing. We came to think of these portfolios as not only metaphorical passports but as 'suitcases' (Canevaro, 1988 cited in Brostrom, 2002), providing documentation and literacy artifacts that value the prior learning and experiences in their lives and that can continue to be used as they continue on their journey. Lenz Taguchi (2006) supports this notion of documentation as an ongoing living artifact:

> From a pedagogical perspective, documentation is not simply to capture or make visible a memory from the past (retrospective), but rather to enable us to analyze and deconstruct, and to be able to make choices for possible learning processes tomorrow (prospective). (p. 260)

We saw the portfolios as having both a retrospective and a prospective role in both settings. We were also interested in how the portfolio books strengthen and support languages and literacies, and in the possibility of interweaving the dispositional approach to learning with the primary school focus on key competencies. To do this we addressed three main questions:

1. Crossing borders between the kindergarten and the local school: how can these relationships be strengthened?

2. Crossing borders across languages and literacies: how can the portfolio books strengthen and support languages and literacies, especially for children for whom English is an additional language?
3. Crossing borders between *Te Whāriki* and the school curriculum: in what ways can we develop continuity from learning dispositions to key competencies?

Chapter 3 begins the investigation of these questions by considering the role of portfolios as tools for enhancing learning across the borders.

CHAPTER 3

Portfolios as tools for enhancing learning across the borders

Views of early childhood assessment and documentation in New Zealand have been dramatically influenced by the national early childhood curriculum. The theoretical frameworks of *Te Whāriki* emphasise that curriculum is about "reciprocal relationships with people, places and things" (Ministry of Education, 1996, p. ix), Carr (2001), with early childhood teachers from a number of different types of provision, explored alternative assessment models and in doing so, introduced Learning Stories as an assessment practice. As a form of formative assessment, Learning Stories focus on the relationship between learner and context, documenting the interactions of the learner and reflecting the sociocultural view of learning implicit in *Te Whāriki*. Fleer (2002) has commented that Learning Stories, as vignettes of children 'in action' are:

> rich, forward thinking (i.e. assessment for tomorrow) and demonstrate a complexity of moving from and individual to a sociocultural perspective of assessment in early childhood education. This work is at the cutting edge of knowledge construction on assessment in early childhood education. (p.112)

This paradigm shift to assessment as a sociocultural activity supports the use of the portfolio not only as an individual record of learning in one setting, but as an assessment and documentation tool that can cross the borders between settings.

Carr (2001, citing Gipps, 1999), has described the role of Learning Stories and their portfolios as being to:

- document learning over time
- assess students' learning, reflecting their relationships and interactions
- develop self-assessment capacity within the learning process.

We see portfolios within this paradigm shift as "part of a move to design assessment that supports learning and provides more detailed information about students" (Gipps, 1999, p. 368).

Over the course of several years the portfolios at Mangere Bridge Kindergarten have come to mean much more than a formative assessment tool for the children, the teachers and the families. They have developed and changed as the teaching team have learned about assessment and Learning Stories and have developed inclusive practices, recognising that learning and assessment in practice is always a journey in progress. Portfolios are now viewed at Mangere Bridge Kindergarten from a multitude of perspectives, that define them as literacy artifacts and as tools of engagement supporting empowerment, interaction and communication. By connecting the child and family in the border crossings between home and kindergarten, and later between home, kindergarten and school, these portfolios promote "conditions for the possibility of learning" (Gipps, 1999, p. 374). Learning Story assessment practices of noticing, recognising, and responding to key learning events are integral to the teaching and learning in the kindergarten. These practices are used to write narratives included in the children's portfolios and are linked to planning for further teaching and learning. The portfolios present a multi-dimensional perspective of the child as learner.

Portfolios at Mangere Bridge Kindergarten

As the learning journey begins

At the commencement of their kindergarten journey each child has a portfolio created for them, which contains some information filled in by the parent/caregiver, some information contributed by the child in the form of drawings, and information about the kindergarten, the teachers and their interests. A narrative of the first day for each child goes into the child's portfolio, and this story is often the first means of engaging with a child (and their family) and building a relationship to create a sense of belonging in the new environment. This first day at kindergarten is recorded as a settling experience. The portfolio invites the parents to tell the teachers what their child said about their first day at kindergarten. Responding to this question, a parent whose older two children had kindergarten portfolios, wrote "Piper loves having her own book [portfolio] which is hers because, she said, 'I been waiting'". During the child's time at kindergarten Learning Stories are added to the portfolio (individual, group and personalised group stories) along with art work, children's work, kindergarten events and child and family contributions.

The portfolios are stored in a book box at the children's height. The box includes dividers, which are colour coded, named and have a photograph across the top so that children can access their own portfolios.

If the portfolio has gone home, the divider is useful as a place holder and also as a space to store further stories until they can be added to the book. Children constantly access their portfolios, often carrying them around during the session. They can be seen using them to engage other children, parents, whānau and even visitors in conversation. A protocol around ownership of the portfolios was developed at the kindergarten: children must ask the owner of the portfolio for permission if they want to read it. This protocol was later transferred by the children into the school environment and was important for the success of the portfolios as a transition tool.

A taonga[11] for parents and children

Planning and assessment with children within the kindergarten is dependent on establishing a relationship in order to build on previous learning, family practices, and established and emerging interests. As the portfolios move between kindergarten and home, contributions are added at home as well. The family's comments, stories and photos in the portfolios record family experiences and events, celebrations, holidays, special friends and visitors. Parents consider the kindergarten portfolios to be valued family taonga recording their child's learning and important experiences in their lives and the lives of the family. The ongoing nature of this attachment became clear when a kindergarten teacher met a previous kindergarten child (by this time in primary school Year 6) and her mother at the shops on a Sunday afternoon, and the first comment was about how they still love her "kindy book" and the child volunteered immediately, "I had it out last week actually".

During an interview another parent commented:

> you know I love her kindy book … [hugging it to her chest] … she always loved coming here … and seeing that book you can see why … you know some of the interesting stuff you guys have done for her and helped her grow … I'd rather keep it up on the shelf because you can't replace these things. (Parent interview, project year 3)

---

11 Taonga: The Māori term for a treasure.

This parent recognised the valuable learning for her child that had occurred during her kindergarten days and she often responded in the portfolio, as did many others.

The portfolio was highly valued in Kaitlin's family also. It was regularly read at home and returned to kindergarten with insights for the reader about her home life. Kaitlin frequently revisited her portfolio at the kindergarten as well. Kaitlin showed expertise at reading the visual language that her family had contributed. The illustrations were the prompts for her, enabling her to recite whole chunks of the written language and to revisit her learning.

> **TEACHER REFLECTION**
>
> I sat down with Kaitlin, who was reading her portfolio on her own. She started telling me about what was in her book, recalling a visit to the Skytower, stories about her friend Brooke and various other events. I was struck at how well she knew the book. There are several pages in her book that have contributions from home. Kaitlin's mum and dad have done the writing and Kaitlin has drawn the pictures. Given that some of the contributions are from a year or so ago, I was absolutely amazed when Kaitlin was able to tell me what each story was about. She had all the details correct. I suppose I shouldn't be surprised as they are HER stories! These particular stories were without the visual aid of photographs, just writing and her own illustrations (which in some cases were quite small). Her level of knowledge is very enlightening, and illustrates the significance portfolios have for recording events in the lives of children.
> (Teacher reflection, project year 2)

This experience with the portfolio was later repeated for her brother, Christian, when he began attending this kindergarten. His book contained photos and stories of attendance at family weddings, among lots of other events, highlighting his experience as a competent ring bearer and Samoan dancer. These events contributed to the interests that Christian had in the kindergarten, revealing him to be both a learner and a teacher. The photos provided from home in his portfolio provided visual models for Christian, to share and to show other children how to perform the dance steps.

Teacher portfolios

The teachers also constructed their own portfolios that contain stories and photos of both their professional and home life. They are stored in amongst the children's portfolios in alphabetical order in the upright box. These teacher portfolios originated from an idea about bio-boards from Curtis and Carter (2003). These boards were made to display at the entrance to the kindergarten, where parents sign in, and they are then each converted to a half page of text and photographs to go in every child's portfolio. We felt that if parents were able to access information about the teacher as a person with interests and passions outside of the kindergarten, it would create a space to build a relationship and sometimes find common ground in interactions. Following on from this, we decided to

develop these bios into an individual portfolio for each adult in the kindergarten, similar to those we had seen at Botany Downs Kindergarten, another Auckland kindergarten. The children constantly access the teacher portfolios, discussing where teachers live, their families, pets and interests outside of the kindergarten. They discuss our photos, investigating the relationships portrayed, and build a picture of the teacher as a learner as well as a participant in the life of the children and families in the kindergarten community.

More recently, William, a toy guinea pig, joined one of the teachers on a holiday in London and began sending emails and photos back from London with Carol. He now has his own portfolio and the children are able to take William for adventures on family holidays, and send photos back to kindergarten, to be displayed and added to William's portfolio. The children are very enamoured of William and his portfolio and it is a wonderful additional way of learning about our families' lives outside of the kindergarten. All of this documentation contributes to the funds of knowledge about the children, families and teachers (Gonzales, Moll & Amanti, 2005). These visual records are highly accessible, able to be read, revisited and shared.

Transitioning with portfolios

A positive sense of self

Discussing what makes a "good" transition, Brooker (2008, pp. 114-115) calls for "an environment of opportunities", and the portfolios took on this role of promoting an environment in which children could engage with others and convey a sense of their own self worth. Ecclestone (2009) reinforces the interwoven nature of assessment and transitions, and suggests that successful transitions require systems of support to empower those involved. One kindergarten parent commented on the value of the portfolios as transition tools: "Their books are wonderful … as a record to take to school, in terms of who they are and what they do" (Parent focus group, project year 2). In addition, a new entrant teacher made the following comment:

> I've noticed that even the most shy of children when they've got their portfolio with them just seem to have this sense of confidence, it's that ownership over something and the fact that the other children in the class are acknowledging their prior learning and lots of rich experiences … it's a really, really useful tool for transition. (Teacher C, interview, project year 3)

Families for whom English is an additional language

In the evolution of the portfolio from assessment tool to transition artifact, the portfolios also fulfilled a multitude of roles for those children and families for whom English is an additional language. Margetts (2007) reported from an Australian research study that children from families where English is an additional language were less likely to have had access to school and school language before their first day of attendance, were less familiar with school, and consequently found transition more difficult. The portfolios, by using visual images, provide ongoing documentation of learning to communicate and connect with all children and families. The use of new technologies that are less reliant on written language has made possible a transformation in the way we interact with children and families. Photos, movies and images convey information in a way that is accessible to families who are not able to spend time in the kindergarten setting and those for whom English is an additional language. Makin, Jones, Diaz and McLachlan (2007) refer to the challenge of connecting with families and validating their experiences in a pluralistic society such as New Zealand. However, the learning story format and the composition of the portfolios negotiate this challenge by communicating using visual images as well as English language-based text. The story about Gaurav in the next paragraph illustrates that families for whom English is an additional language can connect, through photos, with the learning that has happened for their child in the kindergarten setting and to respond in a way that they find comfortable (including in their home language), linking learning between the two settings.

Portfolios go to school

Gaurav uses his portfolio

Gaurav was the first of our case studies, and his transition provided our initial defining moment, our 'Wow moment!' as his school teacher so succinctly put it. The impact on her class and the resulting implications for Gaurav are reported more fully elsewhere (Peters, Hartley, Rogers, Smith, & Carr, 2009). The power of the portfolio for a child for whom English is an additional language was magnified by Gaurav's adaptation of the kindergarten culture of engagement with children into the school new entrant classroom.

The kindergarten culture of engagement—of negotiating relationships through documentation and portfolios with children and adults—was carried over into the school, and in Gaurav's case was evident on a day when one of the kindergarten teachers was present in the new entrant classroom, working with a group of children. Gaurav tried to join the group; however when he could not get the kindergarten teacher's attention he went off to get his kindergarten portfolio, placed it on the lap of the class relieving teacher and opened it to the page where a kindergarten visit to school was reported. His actions indicated that he knew this visiting kindergarten teacher. He was communicating with the school teacher in the way he felt most comfortable, visually, using his portfolio. He had used his portfolio to engage children and unfamiliar adults on numerous occasions during his school transition experience, and, indeed, for many months afterwards.

Portfolios as literacy artifacts

When asked in a focus group of new entrants at school (recently arrived 5-year-olds) what the portfolios were used for at school, they answered as follows:

> L: You use them for reading.
> M: Yeah and for looking at and for reading with a partner or someone has to ask us if they want to read them.
> A: If they want to read someone else's kindy book.
>
> (Children's focus group, project year 2)

These children were part of a culture in the classroom that developed the rule that if you wanted to read a "kindy" book you had to ask the owner. One explanation for this was proposed by the teacher in the room, who thought it had been suggested as a way to keep the books in good condition. However, this rule in the kindergarten, originally a way of maintaining privacy, came to mean that children had ownership of their own portfolio and the interactions that accompanied its use.

It is important to note that the individual portfolios of the children in the kindergarten are highly valued and frequently accessed, but this has to be done with the permission of the owner. They are carried, read and pored over by children as they discuss their learning and experiences with each other, with teachers and with any available adult. Over the period of the research this culture extended to the school setting in many different ways.

Portfolios go to school

Several of the teachers at the schools reported the value of the kindergarten portfolios in the transition process, and used them in interactive and inclusive ways. They began to write Learning Stories to include in the portfolio outlining the school visit experience.

> And when they come for their visit [I was] adding to the portfolio by trying to do a Learning Story, even though I'm not sure what your learning intentions are for Te Whāriki. But even if I just recorded what the children are doing at the school so it could be included in their portfolio and take back to share, so we're keeping that communication going with the kindergarten. (Teacher C, interview, project year 3)

One of these teachers' Learning Stories highlighted the competency of a child at the carpentry table on his first visit to school. This story connected to many other stories in this child's portfolio that illustrated his interest and competence in carpentry and construction. It linked his interests at kindergarten to school and formed the basis for creating a sense of belonging and a context for learning in the new setting.

The teachers encouraged the children and families to transport the portfolios between the kindergarten and the school and to share stories in each setting. In moving between the settings in this way there was a sense in which these portfolios helped to open what Thomson (2002) termed children's "virtual school bags", which are full of various cultural and linguistic resources. The school bag metaphor is similar to Canevaro's (1988, cited in Brostrom, 2002) more tangible "suitcase" of stories, photographs and objects, which help teachers connect to the child's earlier learning. Our aim was to explore practices that allow the contents of all children's suitcases or virtual school bags to be recognised

Manfred found his friends James and Lachlan. He played in the sand tray with the jungle animals and had lots of fun tipping sand over them to bury them. Manfred built things at the wood work table. He knew he had to bang the nails very hard to make them go in as far as possible.

and welcomed in both early childhood and school settings. This involved challenging practices whereby only some children, "those whose resources match those required in the game of education" (Thomson & Hall, 2008, p. 89), get to open their 'virtual school bag' and use what is inside, while for other children their "knowledges, experiences and practices remain invisible and unused at school" (Thomson, 2002, cited in Kamler & Comber, 2005, p. 6). In addition, we sought ways to add learning to the virtual school bags, or backpacks, in the hope that this would carry not only across tasks but also across contexts (or borders). Children were empowered by being allowed to open the suitcase/virtual school bag by accessing their portfolios at a time of their choosing and in a way they were comfortable with.

Gaurav's new entrant teacher welcomed the books into the classroom and reported:

> I would turn around at all times of the day and hear little murmurings and laughing and there would be pockets of children sitting around this little boy with his kindy book. (School teacher interview, project proposal stage)

However, this entitled and interactive use of the portfolio was not universal. As an example of the difficulty of handing a precious 'treasure' into someone else's care, one parent perceived a lack of appreciation for her daughter's portfolio in a new entrant room. She reported that the teacher said, "Oh that's lovely, put it in the box, we'll bring it out at news". The parent commented:

> The importance of it wasn't really, I was going to say, appreciated. So ... I left it there but I wanted to go back and get it because to me it's precious ... if it wasn't going to be recognised by the teacher as a precious thing ... so [at the] end of the day I whipped it out of there. (Parent interview, project year 3)

On another occasion, however, a new entrant teacher created a similar portfolio, making a school version for a child, Jayden:

> He really valued it, and every day he would go and read it and chose a friend to read it with. So I made him, um, a similar sort of portfolio which started from his first day at school, and you know we talked about and took photos of activities that he was doing at school and then [I] got him to dictate a little story about then, which I typed out. (Teacher G, interview, project year 2)

This teacher identified Jayden's attachment to his portfolio as a learning opportunity, particularly for literacy. In creating a book in a similar format and size, she supported him in his literacy learning, while the book and its use identified him as a learner in the school situation. Creating a similar portfolio at school builds on the use of portfolios and keeps them connected to the new environments. This potentially addresses the concerns expressed by some (children and adults) that children need to leave their kindergarten days behind them and move on. When five-year-old Myrrin was asked if the portfolio book was still at school, some time after having started school, she very confidently replied, "No, because I came to school last year. I've been here longer. I took my book home because I know everything now" (Child conversation, project year 2). For Myrrin, the portfolio had been a valuable transition tool, providing a means of interaction and, a positive image of herself as a learner that was no longer needed as she had established herself fully in the new setting. She had "moved on" and now saw herself as a school pupil.

For some children, for whatever reason, the portfolio did not come to school. The primary school teachers acknowledged the reluctance parents might feel in parting with such a unique and precious document in case it was damaged. One teacher reported, "I can think of two cases at the moment, where the portfolio is such a family treasure that they want to keep it at home" (Teacher B, interview, project year 2). However, teachers in both sectors frequently looked at ways of addressing any reluctance families felt in letting the portfolios come to and stay at school by indicating in very real ways that these artifacts were treasured by teachers too. The kindergarten teachers handed on the portfolios to graduating children in a named kete[12] to protect them, and one of the schools built a specially designed wooden "tree" for the kete to hang on. There was a range of views about how to store the portfolios in the school classrooms, however, and the mode of storage appeared to influence their effective use as a belonging, learning and literacy artifact. Reflecting that she was unsure how to foster greater sharing of portfolios, one teacher commented:

> I don't know how we do that ... part of it is the parents wanting to look after these portfolios and they are precious and somehow we need to say, "Yes we value them because we've had these trees made", but they really aren't being used. (Teacher B interview, project year 3)

In contrast, another teacher thought the portfolios were being used more since they were brought in the kete: "I think now that we've got them in the kete, they're more special, they're better used now" (Teacher G interview, project year 3). There may be other factors beyond the storage issues that were affecting their use, but ensuring the portfolios were easily accessible did seem to be important. Teacher interest and attitude was crucial.

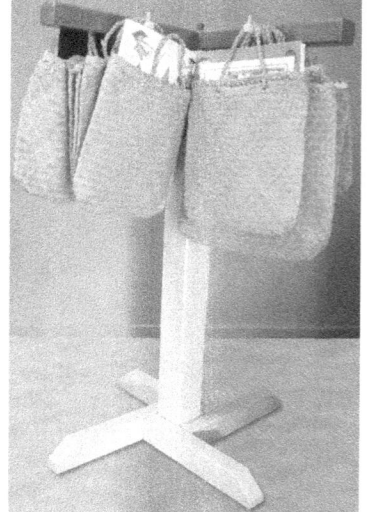

In discussion with teachers during some of our presentations we have heard that some early childhood centres make two portfolios and some are investigating (as we are) the possibility of making an additional, digital portfolio, so that parents and families have copies on a DVD. Currently, as a simple form of backup we give each family

---

12 Kete: The Māori term for a woven basket

a DVD containing all the photos taken of the child taken during their time at kindergarten. We are working on a way to include all the stories written as well, as an additional and more comprehensive backup to the portfolio. These ideas would seem to meet the concerns of parents who consider their child's portfolio to be an irreplaceable treasure and one they wish to keep with their family mementos. Parents may be reassured that the portfolio can not only go to school but can also spend some time at school as a transition tool—and as a contribution to learning at school

Concluding comments

Sociocultural assessment practices are by nature extremely complex and shape a child's formation of identity within that early learner's context (Fleer, 2002). Gipps (1999) writes about assessment and identity:

> Because of the public nature of much questioning and feedback, and the power dynamic in the teacher–student relationship, assessment plays a key role in identity formation. The language of assessment and evaluation is one of the defining elements through which young persons form their identity, for school purposes at least … If identity is concerned with persuading others and oneself about who one is, the judgement of others is crucial. (pp. 282–283)

This contextual notion of identity is reinforced by Brooker (2008), who notes that a child may be secure and comfortable in one setting, but a change of setting may result in the child feeling less able or competent. In our view, and in our experience, the portfolios currently in use within the early childhood sector contribute to the child's identity of themselves as a competent and confident learner, and can positively influence the way children transition into a new setting.

CROSSING the BORDER

CHAPTER 4

Mutually interesting projects

We were able to develop relationships with the local schools in a range of different ways. One of these was through the development of mutually interesting projects. The New Zealand early childhood curriculum document, *Te Whāriki*, emphasises "the critical role of socially and culturally mediated learning and of reciprocal and responsive relationships for children with people, places and things" (Ministry of Education, 1996, p. 9). With the goal of promoting collaborative relationships between early childhood education environments, families and schools, a 10-year strategic plan for early childhood education (*Ngā Huarahi Arataki*, Ministry of Education, 2002) emphasised promoting greater understanding of the differences in pedagogy and curriculum between early childhood and primary educational facilities. It also promotes working towards smoother transitions for children and their families, including those for whom English is an additional language. In seeking to address these important goals, the research team sought to develop projects that met the needs of the participants in our setting. We wanted to develop processes and ideas that could straddle the borders between settings.

With these ideas in mind, we began to work on fostering cross-sector relationships through joint projects. As the kindergarten and local schools worked together, the tools and resources that were developed involved both parties. Projects were developed based on mutual engagement, joint enterprise and the generation of a shared repertoire. These are the three distinct dimensions encompassed in Wenger's notion of a community of practice (Wenger, 1998, p. 73). Our collaborative actions were negotiated together. We drew on our own competence and the competence of others, taking into account the perspectives of all the participants and creating resources that resulted in common practices. Wenger (1998) stresses that a community of practice draws on and strives to retain the unique qualities of each party, acknowledging their diversity, and that rather than seeking to standardise practice among contributors seeks to establish a coherent and symbiotic relationship among the participants. These ideas underpin the notion of working on joint projects, and building relationships, while progressing the interests and aims of all the participating parties.

Chapter 3 documented the use of children's portfolios as a tool of engagement in the new entrant classroom. Building on this existing use of portfolios and the longstanding relationships established with the teachers at one school in our community, we sought to discover other possibilities to support children, their families and teachers at kindergarten and both local schools during the transition process. In developing other ideas, the schools became key partners in joint projects, and we were able to utilise their teachers' expertise to work collaboratively to further strengthen the relationships. The emerging relationships with the schools led to dialogue around other projects of interest, and the ways in which we could collaborate on supporting children's transition to school.

A transition to school photo display board at the kindergarten

One of the earliest transition projects at kindergarten was a transition to school photo display board. This display board is a feature in the kindergarten that connects photos and information about the nearby schools to photos of the kindergarten children. Each side of this moveable display board shows one of the two schools, and includes pictures of the entrance to the schools, the principal, deputy, office staff, junior school teachers and school uniform. Under the photos of the classroom teachers the kindergarten children place their own photos when they commence their pre-entry visits to school. This means they have a ready reference to their first school teacher, and to the children from kindergarten who will also be in their new entrant class. As one school teacher noted, "our pictures are up there and I'm sure that helps the children" (Teacher A interview, project year 3). The photographs of children from kindergarten who move on to schools other than our two main schools are featured across the bottom of one side of the display board, and in our case equate to only a handful of children over a year.

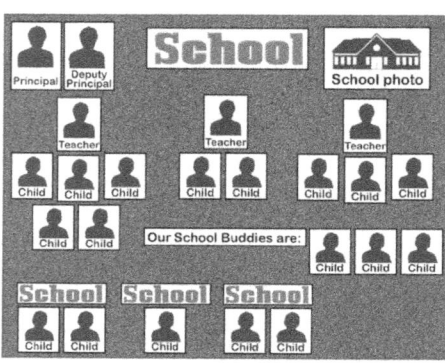

We have seen many ways in which this idea can be tailored to suit individual contexts, and we also understand that this project might need to be modified in those early childhood centres where children

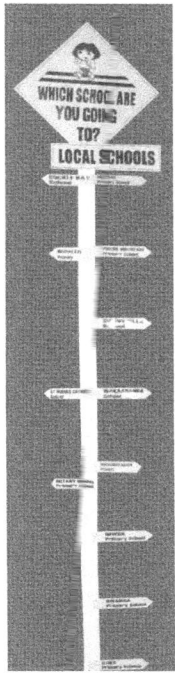

are destined for a catchment of many schools. An interesting example we have seen in another kindergarten, Pigeon Mountain Kindergarten, was the the use of a model AA sign, with each of the 12 schools named on an arrow and children's photos underneath the sign naming their future school.

The display board is a focal point of conversation for children with their families, their peers and their kindergarten teachers. Photos of children who have gone to school over past years are kept in books, and these are accessed often by the children themselves when they return to collect siblings or friends, and by kindergarten children who search for friends and siblings who have moved on to school. For example, each day Sam would bring out the book and sit at the writing table, turning each page slowly, looking at each photo until he found the photos of his brother and cousins. Pointing at the photos he would say, "Look Frances, that's David and that's Sione and look at Ofa" (Learning Story, project year 1).

Later, when we introduced the idea of school buddies (see Chapter 6), the photos of the school buddies were added to the school board, creating an additional link between kindergarten children and their school buddies. This provides another point of connection for kindergarten children, individually and collectively, as their move to school approaches. They can often be found sitting in front of the school board looking at the photos and discussing their buddies:

> Josh: This is my buddy, who is yours? Oh yeah, yours is Richard, eh?
> Frankie: I'm going to that school.
> Taine: Yeah, we all are, eh.
> (Children's conversation, project year 3)

The visual nature of the school board allows children to access the information independently, at any time of the day. This is an example of how the environment can play a part in enabling informed transitions to be the subject of positive and animated conversations from early on in the children's kindergarten experience.

The 'Welcome to School' DVD project

The history of mutual engagement with one school in our community enabled us to discuss the development of a resource about transition. This idea was inspired by research

elsewhere that sought to understand children's ideas about starting school, such as the Starting School Research Project. In this project Dockett and Perry (2003) investigated children's transition to school over several years, asking children to photograph their experience of visiting school. These photos were used to understand the experience from the children's perspective.

As outlined in Chapter 1 we had been involved with the Educational Leadership Project research prior to our Centre of Innovation project. This early work had involved a small number of children taking cameras on school visits and capturing what was important to them. Through the photos and resulting conversations with the children it became clear that what was important for the children was relationships with friends and family, along with aspects of the school environment such as where to hang your bag, the location of the toilets and the playground. Another of the teaching teams in that Educational Leadership Project developed a book that was given to children moving into new entrant classrooms. Their book contained similar details that the children had identified as significant, such as pictures of where to hang your bag, what the office looked like and where the toilets were.

Our idea was to develop a movie that enabled children at kindergarten to see and hear what children at school valued about school and what they thought kindergarten children should know before coming to school. In the planning stage the 'Welcome to School' DVD was envisaged as an information tool, giving a virtual tour of one of the nearby schools and introducing the principal, teachers and specific staff whom the children and their families were likely to encounter in their early interactions with the school. We surveyed the kindergarten families to determine the most appropriate format for a resource to share. The results revealed that 98 percent of families had a DVD player or computer for playing DVDs.

At the same time as we were thinking about this, the participating school became involved in an ICT project, and a team of five Year 5 schoolchildren (aged 8–9), four of whom just happened to be ex-Mangere Bridge Kindergarten children, needed a project. Along with the school and these children, we (the Mangere Bridge Kindergarten teachers) began the process of making a short movie about school. Meetings took place between the kindergarten teachers and the school team, which consisted of the deputy principal and the five children. Ideas were discussed at school, and the team then visited kindergarten to talk to the children to find out what they wanted to know about school. Storyboards were drawn up, sequences established and filming started, with the schoolchildren in charge. The outcome was a DVD which introduced key features of the physical environment of the school and some of the key staff members. It also included information the children thought was important, like not running out of the gates. The schoolchildren involved in making the DVD also offered insights into school practices that new entrant children would experience on commencing school, such as visiting the hall for assembly.

They were also able to share their views about school, and why they liked it. One school teacher commented:

> I think the DVD was great because the kids did it themselves. It's not world class in terms of editing and filming but we thought it was giving a true story about what was happening because we like to give our kids the responsibility of doing things. (Teacher E, interview, project year 3)

There were challenges for both sides during this project. One significant issue was coordinating meetings between the two settings at times that suited both parties. Other challenges were changes in the children's team, with some children moving on or away from school, and changes in staff at the school. These changes meant re-editing the footage, at which point we realised this could not be a one-off production and that there would be further challenges in keeping the material up to date:

> We keep having hiccups with that because we keep changing staff and we had a different principal last year so it's getting that [new version] up and running and using it. (Teacher D, interview, project year 3)

Changes in staff at the kindergarten also required catch-up time for new members to get up to speed with progress. However, such challenges are never insurmountable in a willing relationship, and the movie sequence began to take shape. The finished product was then made available to children and their families at kindergarten when they indicated that this was their school of choice. Copies were also given to the school to offer to all children and families enrolling at the school. The process of making the DVD enabled an already strong relationship to become even stronger, through the collaboration and consultation that took place on the joint project. The information technology [IT] aspect also offered a new dimension to the relationship with the families of the kindergarten, who were able to utilise this visual resource in their own settings at home, facilitating further conversations about and around the transition to school. It also provided a school project within the technology curriculum and added to the school's information and communications technology [ICT] research file.

Feedback from children and their families on their use of the DVD supported the notion that it was a valuable resource that supported children and their families to prepare for the transition to school. One child said, "I liked [seeing] Mrs W's class … I saw the boys and girls telling the teacher's names, the teacher's rooms and the teacher's [room] numbers" (Child interview, project year 2). Parents used it to help children become familiar with people and places at the school. Parent feedback included, "It was all helpful … [to see] which one is the teacher, [to know] the teacher's name, and know where the toilets are" (Parent interview, project year 3).

Another parent said:

> It was really good, because I think they forget, you know, they hear people's names and all those different things and it all gets all muddled in their minds and he and I sat down … we sat down with popcorn and watched it and it

really felt [like] oh, that's right, that's that person, and it just helped all those connections, and I think he felt a bit more comfortable … even just showing where the toilets are, you know things like that, it all gets a bit blurred. (Parent focus group, 1 year post project)

An informal conversation with another parent revealed an unexpected advantage. As a parent for whom English was an additional language, she valued hearing the teachers' names pronounced so that she felt confident about using them correctly herself.

In addition to the school visits made by groups of kindergarten children and teachers (seen as separate from the individual pre-entry visits made by children and their families), the DVD meant that families could familiarise themselves with people, places and things related to the school environment before starting pre-entry visits. Dialogue in the familiar settings of kindergarten and home opened up opportunities for further discussion around the whole process of moving to school. This enabled children and their families to start school empowered by a familiarity with the setting, thus minimising the effects of the differences between the settings of kindergarten and school.

An added bonus was the positive experience for the schoolchildren involved in developing this resource. As well as working with the kindergarten children and developing the DVD, there were other unexpected benefits, as the older schoolchildren began to take more interest in welcoming the new children to their school, including inviting the kindergarten children to student-led 'Jump Jam' sessions at school.

Early childhood and primary links group

The process of fostering positive relationships between kindergarten and school in the local community led to deeper reflection on the ways in which our progress could be communicated to the wider community for the benefit of their own local context. This led us to establish an Early Childhood and Primary Links (ECPL) group, where representatives from early childhood and school settings in our community came together on a regular basis to discuss mutually interesting topics and the influence of pedagogy and practice in each setting. Initially we shared our experiences in establishing and strengthening relationships, and acknowledged the critical importance of relationships in developing sustainable and beneficial communities of practice. We were able to offer critical insight into how the collaborative nature of developing transition resources strengthens relationships and supports children's transition to school.

In light of the interest shown by early years practitioners in our community, we continued to host this gathering, arranging facilitators for subsequent meetings with a focus on topics of interest to both early childhood and school practitioners. The aim was to explore cross-sector issues, and coming together for a specific purpose resulted in wider dialogue about practice and pedagogy. As one school teacher noted, "It was really interesting listening to the conversations and the views from other schools ... 'oh, is that what happens in other schools'" (Teacher D, interview, project year 3). Another teacher commented:

> I thought, "This is good because I'm learning and we're not coming here [to visit the kindergarten] to tell." Yes we're opening up a partnership or a dialogue so I think it's going to get stronger. (Teacher C, interview, project year 3)

Having a forum at which practitioners from a variety of settings could engage in dialogue about learning and teaching proved a useful way of sharing knowledge and improving understanding about the different models of practice in our community. In addition, visits to kindergarten by teachers from the schools have led to a better understanding of the early childhood programme and environment, and as a result they have incorporated ideas from kindergarten into their own programmes at school, such as purchasing carpentry tables like those at kindergarten for use in the new entrant school environment. We commented in Chapter 3 about one of the school teacher's Learning Stories highlighting the competence of a child at carpentry. Learning Stories and carpentry from kindergarten were taken up by the school because they were mutually interesting.

Concluding comments

Through joint projects we established artifacts that crossed boundaries and supported children and families as they transitioned from kindergarten to school. Teachers from both settings worked together without compromising the philosophy of either setting. However, it was equally important to look at the ways in which adjustments could be made in order to best serve the needs of the children and their families. In our case this required, above all, a willingness to accommodate a degree of change in the programmes and practices of each setting. We found that artifacts that are created to support balanced relationships need to be contextually based. In making the first move, teachers need to be prepared to persevere, with the aim of finding a suitable joint project for their community. Brostrom (2007) cites Lave and Wenger (1991), who argue for learning that is woven together and occurs in settings that are linked by "a specific shared, social practice" (p. 63).

Our findings indicate that although the product itself had an important role to play, the relationships that developed as a result became integral to sustaining our community of practice. The consultation and collaboration required between the settings throughout the joint projects offered opportunities for an ongoing partnership, endorsing and validating the learning in both sectors and generating a foundation on which to build stronger relationships.

CROSSING the BORDER

CHAPTER 5

Mutually familiar language, routines and practices

Many of the projects in Chapters 3 and 4 produced artifacts, and these provided transitioning children with language, routines and common practices they could take across the border with them as well as contributing to a sense of familiarity for families. The research project indicated that this knowledge (whether it was of practices, routines or content) paved the way for competent participation in the new setting. As Wenger (1998) notes, "because learning transforms who we are and what we can do, it is an experience of identity" (p. 215). Mutually familiar language, routines and practices that became common to the different settings not only added to the children's learning experiences and development of skills, but also gave children an insight into these new languages, routines and practices, affording a greater sense of participation. In his exploration of communities of practice, Wenger (1998) comments that communities of practice are "a living context that can give newcomers access to competence" (p. 214).

Based on their research in schools, Timperley et al. (2003) have suggested that the professional responsibility of the teachers in early childhood and primary school settings is to offer "*complementary* activities so that children recognise that strategies acquired in the early childhood setting can be applied to school" (p. 33). Where the differences in what happens on either side of the boundaries are blurred in this way, children begin to see opportunities for applying their knowledge and skills in the new setting, adding to their perception of themselves as capable and confident learners.

Nutbrown and Clough (2009) refer to curriculum guidance and statutory requirements in the UK for the early years foundation stage, which state under the heading 'Enabling environment': "When children feel confident in the environment they are willing to try things out, knowing that effort is valued" (p. 192). They claim that practitioners in early years settings who support children to "feel good about themselves, feel positive about the differences they see in other children and are secure in their own sense of place in their early years community" bring about a "sense of inclusivity and belonging" (Nutbrown & Clough, 2009, p. 203). We could see this in the example of Myrrin who, when offered help during an activity on her first school visit, responded confidently to her teacher, "I don't need any help, thank you" (Learning Story, project year 1). Her mother later commented, "I thought that was quite impressive from Myrrin ... she obviously had a confidence there that I wasn't really aware of" (Parent interview, project year 2).

As we saw in Chapter 3, the children's portfolios have many roles. One of these is as a "tool of common knowledge". We found that the ways in which children and families, along with their peers and teachers, entered into conversation about the experiences reported in these books allowed a meeting of minds around what was identified as common knowledge. Through repeated engagement, this common knowledge developed into a shared repertoire for those involved. Opportunities for children to share the knowledge with others were significantly increased through the use of this documentation. Wenger has written about an 'identity of participation', and he comments that "What makes information knowledge—what makes it empowering—is the way in which it can be integrated within an identity of participation" (1998, p. 220).

School visits

Targeted school visits

Initially, regular school visits with the kindergarten children had not been a feature of the relationship with one of the schools in our community. This changed and developed as the partnership strengthened. A contributing factor was the responses to a parent survey that asked what more could be done to support their child's move from kindergarten to school. The majority of parents indicated that kindergarten visits to school would be beneficial. This information was shared with the school, and as a result visits were arranged. At the beginning of each term, the children who will be starting at this school during that term walk to school with a kindergarten teacher and spend time in the classroom they will be going into, participating in the programme for approximately 1 hour. This visit with a kindergarten teacher allows children to visit and explore the new environment with a group of friends before beginning individual visits. It is an example of how visits can be negotiated between the kindergarten and the school, which are additional to the child's pre-entry visits arranged between the school and the parents.

The 'school visit book' resulted from one of these visits to another nearby school. On this occasion the new entrant teacher took her class and the group of visiting kindergarten children on a tour of the school. The tour was

photographed by the accompanying kindergarten teacher and a book was created that documented the different areas of the school, the playground, the toilets, the office, the staff room and the classroom, and included a short commentary on each. This personalised record of the visit, developed with the children, overcame the concern one school teacher expressed about more generalised 'transition books' that adults created for children, which she felt potentially "robbed children of the opportunity to find out for themselves". The children could see themselves in the book and were able to gain confidence by finding out, recording their discoveries and revisiting them later with others. The kindergarten children and their families were thrilled with this record of their visit, and parents found it particularly useful for discussing their own visit and the imminent commencement of school for their children. The kindergarten now makes an individualised book with each group of kindergarten children visiting this school. The school visit book is a useful tool, providing an opportunity for engaging children, families and teachers in dialogue about the routines of school.

Parent feedback included, "I think the biggest thing really has been that we're familiar with the environment and the children know their way round before they get up there" (Parent focus group, project year 2); and "She loved the classroom, she loved the fact that she had already been to visit school and felt quite comfortable there ... she knew where things like the toilets were and that sort of stuff" (Parent interview, project year 2).

General school visits

School visits for children who are nearly 5 often link the children to the specific school they will attend. However, as an extension of previous professional development and collaboration, once a term *all* of the kindergarten teachers and children from the morning session visit one local school. We catch the bus, and then the children are divided into groups of about six and (with adult support in a ratio of 1:3) are placed into the junior classrooms (new entrant to Year 2) for the morning. The children participate in the programme for that time, giving them insight into such things as classroom routines, equipment, the interactions between the teacher and children in that room, and the layout of the classroom environment.

One of the school teachers noted how this session was planned to give a realistic taste of the new entrant programme:

> We used to say, "Great, kindy's coming, wipe the programme for the morning and have the sand and the water and the developmental play out" and then we thought about it and thought particularly for parents coming in as well they're not going to see a true picture of what happens in a new entrant classroom so we have a mixture of that. The teachers tend to do some kind of language experience so they might read a big book and then do some writing and drawing or painting around that so they get a little of school with some development play as well. (Teacher D, interview, project year 3)

Following whole kindergarten visits to school, parents reported that, whether or not their child went on to attend this school, the visits proved to be a useful experience to orient their children's (and their own) thinking when talking about what happens at school.

Although some families whose children would not be attending this school didn't think these visits were valuable, others saw the value and made comments such as, "I think it was really good … to see the teachers, see the … size … I think the size of the school—it's quite overwhelming"; and "[It is helpful to see what school is] not just from the outside but physically being in it … being with the kids and the teacher and the routine" (Parent focus group, Project year 2). Children have often commented during these visits that a particular practice or type of equipment is "just like at kindy". The kindergarten teachers have also found these visits valuable. We include songs, stories, terminology and learning themes from school in our practice at kindergarten to support and strengthen our programme and to further add to the compatibility of learning between settings.

Family expectations and school visits

One of the challenges that can occur in the transition process is that parents are sometimes dealing with their own outdated or negative experiences of school (Brostrom, 2002). Our research highlighted this challenge: "A lot of parents are quite nervous that their only reflection of school is their secondary schooling, which a lot of people didn't enjoy" (Teacher D, interview, project year 3). One parent felt that the school visits helped her overcome these issues: "I think I was more worried about it from [child's] point of view because I hated [school] so much ... I absolutely hated school, and my mother hated my teacher, and I hated my school, and it was awful" (Parent focus group, project year 2).

Playground book

In discussing further possibilities for sustaining the relationship with one school, the idea of a playground book was discussed. Parents had shared their concerns about children's uncertainty during break times. Some reported that their child "didn't like it cos he's got no friends and he said he was crying at lunch time", and "they seem to come out of the classroom and just run, so [if] you're running with somebody at the time, it's fine, but if you're not, you're going to be left behind" (Parent focus group, project year 2). Children from both schools also reported feelings of uncertainty in the playground in the early stages of their transition to school: "I don't like going in the playground here ... because it's scary" (Child interview, project year 2); and "the playground ... for M it was very daunting" (Parent interview, project year 2).

To combat these feelings, we discussed how a book detailing the options for children at break times could be shared with visiting and new entrant children. We thought that children who were prepared with prior knowledge in this way would have a better time adjusting to specific new routines and practices at school. As Teacher A noted, the aim is for children to feel that the transition to school is "something new and different but it's something I'm really capable of doing and it's really exciting" (Teacher A, interview, project year 3). Time constraints precluded further development of this idea, but the production of the school visit book has addressed some of the concerns raised by parents. The relationships formed through the buddy programme, which is the subject of the next chapter, have also led to children feeling more supported in the playground.

Information pamphlets and parent packs

From the feedback we received from parents in surveys, focus groups and interviews, we identified several areas in their children's transition to school where parents felt unsupported. These related mainly to the availability of information on specific aspects of the programme and the transition process. What we learnt from this feedback influenced how we shared information on the child's transition to kindergarten, as well as for the move to school. We responded by developing pamphlets that provide the essential information (with photos), in bite-sized portions, rather than handing parents several typewritten pages. These

are made available at different times. Parents receive the pamphlet *Welcome to the Waiting List* when they first add their child's name to the waiting list, and on starting kindergarten in the afternoon they receive a folder which contains:

1. *Welcome to the Afternoon Session*
2. *Food Policy*
3. *Clothing*
4. *Parent Help*
5. *Portfolios*

On moving to the morning session they receive further pamphlets:

6. *Welcome to the Morning Session*
7. *Excursions*
8. *Food Policy*
9. *Nearly Five*
10. *First Days at School*
11. pamphlets relating to aspects of the curriculum (e.g., literacy, clay).

Nearly Five and *First Days at School* relate in particular to the transition to school. The *Nearly Five* pamphlet details the parents' responsibilities for enrolling their child at school and the kindergarten practices for the child's last day at kindergarten. *First Days at School* was written in consultation with each contributing school and provides parents with a brief synopsis of the procedure for the first days at school, including any expectation of parent involvement and a general timetable of the classroom programme.

These pamphlets are the result of information shared in parent focus groups and were designed to address many of the concerns that had been raised by parents. For example, when parents were asked what they would have liked to

know prior to their child's first day of school, their responses included "from a parent point of view, what [happens] on that first day, what was expected from us" and "I probably would have liked to have known more about how long I could have stayed in the class … it was all a bit, sort of, overwhelming … because I didn't want to overstay my welcome" (Parent focus group, project year 2). Another parent commented that they would have liked "a little bit more communication about what actually happens on that first day" (Parent focus group, project year 2). The pamphlets are provided when a child first begins morning kindergarten, between 6 to 8 months before starting school. This may seem too early, but most parents responded, when asked about receiving information about school, that they would have liked this information a lot earlier than they had previously received it.

The school phonics DVD

As the research progressed we acknowledged the need to create a resource unique to each school that would strengthen and sustain the emerging relationships but still support successful learning and transition for the children. During the establishment and early filming of the *Welcome to School* DVD at one school, we were looking for an idea that would meet the particular needs of the other local school. During initial discussions with the school management and staff, we noted the importance of their phonics programme in the new entrant classrooms. The significance of this programme was also evident in feedback from parent focus groups, informing us that the children in the class do the phonic alphabet "every day" (Parent focus group, Project year 2).

The phonics DVD was initially devised as a strategy to establish a relationship with this school, because it was clear that they "had a focus on phonological processing" (Kindergarten teacher reflection, project year 2). We felt this was a way to signal our commitment to the school, indicating that we viewed children's transition to the school as worthy of collaborative attention. Discussion over a period of time led to two teachers from the school being invited to kindergarten to demonstrate their daily phonics routine. This was recorded and later edited into a DVD for kindergarten children and their families. The visuals from the phonics chart were also made up into tactile resources for use in the kindergarten (as matching games, guessing games and for use in other literacy activities), and to be used in playful ways by the children.

We also undertook our own professional development around phonics to further our knowledge about the specific programme that was used in the school. This led us to develop ways to incorporate phonics in many different forms within our programme. As a teaching team we were challenged to find ways to use this specific phonics system in the kindergarten to allow children to develop a familiarity with it, but in a way that did not compromise our philosophy about teaching and learning. This resulted in deeper reflection on our own practices at kindergarten. In what Wenger (1998) terms a "negotiated enterprise" (p. 78), he acknowledges that it is not essential that everyone believes the same thing in a joint enterprise, but rather that it is communally negotiated.

The strategies we used included phonics cards at mat time, a phonics ABC frieze, ABC puzzles, a phonics DVD, and alphabet charts in different areas around the kindergarten. The children became very familiar with the images, as demonstrated by Ben, who, when he saw the ABC chart at school, commented "[it's] the same as kindy Mum" (Parent focus group, project year 2). The professional development undertaken by the kindergarten teachers at this time also confirmed that many of our current practices and routines were valuable foundation literacy experiences. We firmly believe, as does Nicholson (2005), that "a balance of whole language and phonics appears to produce more positive attitudes to reading than does either whole language or phonics alone" (p. 77). When assimilated into activities that had meaning and purpose for the children, we observed children utilising the phonics resources (matching games, guessing games, alphabet cards) to enhance their existing knowledge and competence.

For the children and families of the kindergarten, who at this stage were not able to access the classroom routines and practices other than through their child's individual pre-entry visits, making the DVD provided an opportunity to gain access to knowledge that was valued by the school. Parents could participate with their child in the process of familiarising themselves with the phonics programme in the new entrant classroom. A survey of parents returned comments such as, "We are happy with the transition now, especially the video of the ABC" (Parent survey, project year 2). The value of families being able to access the information in their own settings was illustrated by a child who said she knew lots of the alphabet "because [cousin] does it" (Child interview, Project year 2).

One teacher expressed concern that the phonics DVD presented ideas out of context:

> Of course we have to teach them letter sound knowledge and of course they're going to have to learn to sit on the mat, but it struck me as being I suppose a little bit artificial in that it won't mean anything to the children until they're in that environment. (Teacher C, interview, project year 3).

Other teachers felt that it was really helpful. One emphasised the value of familiarity; the idea, perhaps, that this artifact might contribute to a sense of belonging:

> I think the way we learn the alphabet sounds with the little actions and the kindergarten children, the first time they see us do it they're so excited that they've seen it before. And so that's very helpful: even if they can only remember one or two, that's very good. (Teacher A, interview, project year 3).

This DVD illustrates a different kind of joint project from the *Welcome to School* DVD, and the follow-on phase needed less collaboration. However, in terms of progressing the emerging partnership, the process played a vital role in demonstrating the kindergarten's commitment to the school, the children and their families in contributing to successful and effective transition. Feedback from an ex-kindergarten child supported our belief that this is the case. After being at school for a short while, Jadzia reported to us, "Do you know at school we do 'A' says 'A', 'a' for apple" [and she made the sign], and 'B' says 'B', 'b' for butterfly—and I know it all. We did it at kindy". Jadzia demonstrated that she knew the practices she learnt at kindergarten were useful and valued in the school setting (Project year 2).

Waste free/zero rubbish

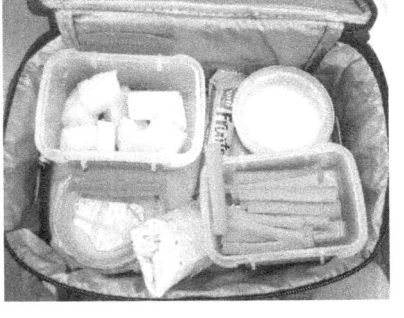

Another initiative that was developed at kindergarten, and that was comparable to school practices, was that of the 'waste free lunch box' or the idea of 'zero rubbish'. Both schools in our research project utilise one or other of these ideas, and at kindergarten we are working on plans to create a sustainable environment.

In a discussion with the principal of one school on introducing the new practices at kindergarten and school, she commented that they had implemented their scheme because "I thought you [the kindergarten] were already doing that" (Project year 3). One of our parents reported being shown a photo of a segregated lunch box packed without wrappers and being told this is what happens at kindergarten: "It's coming from here [kindergarten]" (Parent comment, project year 3). Following a pre-entry visit to the school, a kindergarten child commented, "You know that same notice about to take your rubbish home … they had one too … and they take their rubbish home" (Child interview, project year 3). These comments illustrated to us the impact the strengthening relationship was having on the partnership and practice between the school and the kindergarten.

Concluding comments

The development of the various resources and practices in this chapter was driven by our belief that a familiarity with the language, routines and practices gained through their use would make a difference in the lives of the children and their families. Commenting on the effectiveness of communities of practice as the place where knowledge is shared, interpersonal relationships are developed and projects are negotiated, Wenger (1998) reflects that "such communities hold the key to real transformation—the kind that has real effects on people's lives" (p. 85). The feedback we have received on these tools led us to believe that the children and their families have, as a consequence, entered the school environment more confident and able to manage the many differences in pedagogy and practice.

Communication and dialogue focused on the topic of transition has led to ongoing benefits in terms of kindergarten and school teachers developing greater understanding of their respective settings. This, in turn, has led to further opportunities for those in the kindergarten and school settings to work in tangible, practical and complementary ways. Parents and families have been supported by the sharing of information about the routines and practices across the border into school, as well as being given information on how they can support their child in this move. Through participation in language, routines and practices that are mutually familiar, children are entering the school environment with a sense of some familiarity.

CHAPTER 6

The buddies project

So far we have described some transition practices and projects that we have found to be effective in our communities. In the previous two chapters we identified two categories of these: mutually *interesting* projects and mutually *familiar* language, routines and practices. Many practices and projects belong in both these categories, of course, and the portfolio is an example. The buddies project is another, a project in which children who are nearly-5 at kindergarten and older students from school form relationships in activities that became mutually familiar and mutually interesting. These relationships also have spin-offs for the learning of both age groups—their wellbeing, belonging, exploration, communication and contributions.

This focus on strengthening relationships in the transition to school aligns with the introductory statement in *Te Whāriki* (Ministry of Education, 1996), which places the responsibility with the community for opportunities to foster new learning, to make connections across time and place, and to establish different kinds of relationships. The ability to form meaningful relationships is crucial to later school careers (Dockett & Perry, 2001). Research in New Zealand (Peters, 2003) and Australia (Margetts, 2002) indicates there is a complex relationship between academic performance and peer relationships. Saracho and Spodek (2003) point out that transition involves an ability to learn to adapt, and that children may need social support to do so. Children who enter school with strong communication skills thrive. They are confident and self-assured, adept at making friends, persistent, creative and excited about learning. Brostrom (2005) identifies these as qualities that children acquire through play, and suggests children who are good at pretending are likely to be good at making friends. Knowing how to initiate and maintain a friendship is an important skill that will help children make and keep friends as they enter school (Segal, 2004). The crucial link between relationships and learning is identified by Hamre and Pianta (2007): "If children feel uncomfortable or disconnected from the social environment in the classroom … the potential of the effects of the curriculum are unlikely to be realised" (p. 51).

Central to this issue of children feeling comfortable in their new environment are holistic transition programmes and practices that include opportunities for children to develop friendship skills. Children's peers are highly significant in providing effective support and helping children to feel comfortable in new settings (Dockett & Perry, 2005; Margetts, 2002; Peters, 2003). Clearly the challenge in holistic transition programmes for all children is *how* to facilitate the building of friendships and develop the ability to make and keep friends in order to provide a connection across the two settings. In their writing, Margetts (2002) and Dockett and Perry (2005) both introduce the idea of peer support programmes, or mentoring 'buddy' programmes. Buddy programmes are able to create a climate in which children can be agents of their own transitions through direct experience interacting with a significant other over a period of time.

According to Corsaro (2005), friendships developed in play serve the purpose for children of appropriating and extending social knowledge and developing social identity. He takes this notion further and argues that these skills lead to skills useful in later life. It seems clear, therefore, that play with peers as an agent for transition to school is a useful concept. Playing with peers one has already built a relationship with has the potential to contribute to feelings of belonging—feeling comfortable in a situation that is new, but where there are established relationships. Additional support for this idea of play as a vehicle for furthering learning, and consequently as a transition tool, comes from Kagan and Lowenstein (2004).

This idea is expanded further by Brostrom (2005), who suggests that playing with an older and more competent child supports the transmission of understanding about the transition to school. According to Brostrom, play with an older child "can serve as a transition tool which contributes to children's thinking" (p. 5). He states that children cope better in situations where they can count on support from those they feel are friends. Children who feel comfortable have a more robust sense of belonging and are able to transfer knowledge from one setting to another, which has an impact on their academic learning. They see themselves as more competent because they are challenged to act and think beyond their own level as they learn more about being a school child and how to act like a school child.

Parents in Peters' (2003) study felt that a buddy programme would be particularly effective for children who have no older siblings at school. This is further supported by research by Corsaro and Molinari (2005) and Mapa, Sauvao and Podmore (2000), who found that having siblings at school does indeed make transition smoother. The parents in the Peters (2003) study felt that a buddy would be particularly helpful to support the new child during lunchtimes in the playground, a time and place that has been identified as extremely stressful for some children when they start school. The buddy would be in a substitute role of older sibling and provide similar support. However, Peters also suggests that the development of friendships should not be left to chance, and this would suggest that a buddy project should be contextually based and inclusive of all children in the transition to school, not just those who have no siblings in the school.

Tuakana/teina relationships

In the New Zealand context, the concept of a mentoring situation that is specific to New Zealand and to the bicultural early childhood curriculum document *Te Whāriki* (Ministry of Education, 1996) is the tuakana/teina relationship (Tangaere, 1998). Tuakana/teina is a Māori term that refers to the relationship between an older (tuakana) person and a younger (teina) person, one that is specific to teaching and learning. Originally the tuakana would have been the most senior family member, the "repository of the knowledge and information" (Pere, 1982, p. 46), who would hold the responsibility for passing on this knowledge and information to younger generations. Pere (1982), in discussing Māori learning concepts, suggests that as family ties have been weakened, and maintaining and retaining traditions has become more difficult, so the concept has been formally included into Māori ways of learning and adapted within New Zealand learning communities.

Bird and Drewery (2000) write that this distinctly New Zealand Māori view of a peer support relationship is one that is in place in a variety of educational settings and age ranges, with particularly successful outcomes for children learning to read. In explaining the relationship of tuakana/teina, McFarlane, Glynn, Grace, Penetito and Bateman (2008) outline that the older person has a responsibility to share knowledge and skills with the younger person. Tangaere (1998) adds that "the concept of tuakana/teina operates through the dual concept of ako. The word ako means to learn as well as to teach" (p. 114). In other words, this Māori method of teaching and learning, which involves an older, more knowledgeable person supporting a younger, less knowledgeable person, exactly fits a transition mentoring approach. Ako is linked to concepts of whānau (extended family), belonging and nurturing, and these philosophical beliefs are woven through and have come to inform curriculum in New Zealand, especially in the early years (Tangaere, 1998).

Children learn school social behaviour through forming relationships that involve negotiation, adjustments and understanding peer culture. In the tuakana/teina relationship, extended to the transition experience, the school child is able to model language and behaviours acceptable in school situations, talk about what happens in a classroom, demonstrate positive learning attitudes, and become a friendly face within the new setting (including potentially stressful lunchtimes). In the Māori view, the tuakana/teina relationship extends the mentoring relationship to include fostering a sense of belonging, and also nurturing and caring for the wellbeing of the younger child.

It is worth noting that the tuakana/teina roles are interchangeable, and that the teacher can at times be the learner and vice versa. The possibility of transposing roles supports the notion that being a mentor has learning outcomes for the older child, as was found by the Australian buddy project (Dockett & Perry, 2001). This study found that buddy programmes incorporate learning aims and outcomes for both groups. The older children practised leadership and mentoring skills (and moved beyond a focus on themselves and their own needs and wants), while the younger children were supported as they became familiar with a new environment. Dockett and Perry found that successful transitions are based on social skills and a series of responsive and reciprocal relationships. They conclude that the threefold aims of the project—to promote a positive start for new entrant children, to provide leadership and mentoring training and experience for older primary children, and to promote the concept of transition to school as a community event—were largely met in the Australian project. They are also highly relevant for understanding the outcomes of a programme designed for the New Zealand context, where transition is a particularly individual experience.

The buddies project begins

At the later stages of our research, as we continued to review the relationships and resources we had built with the schools, an idea that had been proposed by a parent about school children being buddies for kindergarten children began to take shape. We were discussing further project ideas and this parent commented that "Kids always have adults telling them what to do; wouldn't it be great if kids told kids about school" (Parent interview, project year 3). This resonated with us and reminded us of a 2003 report we had read, about a small project that linked children with special needs with an older child at a school on the West Coast of New Zealand. We felt that we would like to include all transitioning children in a buddy project, and so we made an appointment to meet with one of our local junior school teaching teams.

When we reported the comment from this parent to the school teachers and discussed initiating a new project, the school was keen to foster relationships between Year 5 children and kindergarten children. It was agreed that Year 5 children would be chosen because these children are still at the primary school the following year and can continue to support a new entrant if required. (In the New Zealand system, a Year 6 child would have moved on the next year to an Intermediate school). Also, it would be effective leadership training, since these Year 5 students would become the oldest in the school (Year 6) the following year.

On starting at this school, all children are paired with a Year 5 student, who becomes their 'read-to' buddy. In this programme, the older child selects appropriate picture books for their new entrant child and reads to them each day for 10–15 minutes after the first break. This read-to programme was already in place in the school when we approached the teachers. It was proposed that the kindergarten buddy relationship would continue into the school as the 'read-to' buddy relationship.

The buddies project initially involved the Year 5 child visiting kindergarten once a week, spending time on different activities with their kindergarten buddy and getting to know them, so that on starting school the new entrant child has a big buddy at school they already know well. The school child then continues the relationship as that child's school read-to buddy. At the outset of the programme, and now each time we have a new buddy group, the prospective buddies visit the kindergarten at a time when there are no kindergarten children present, to familiarise themselves with the environment and talk with the kindergarten teachers about what being a buddy will involve.

The kindergarten teachers prepare a portfolio for each school buddy, including a job description, contract and ethics form, and also write down the qualities the buddies will need to display when in the kindergarten environment. This mentor contract emphasises the importance of "getting to know your buddy, behaving responsibly, being a friend and being a positive role model for your school".

Pawan (Year 5) was heard encouraging a newly selected school buddy before a visit: "It's so cool. You'll have lots of fun but you have to really get to know your buddy" (1 year post project). Another example of positive mentoring occurred when Levi (Year 5 school buddy) and Kiana were putting their learning stories into their portfolios together, and Levi said, "You don't have to be shy because when you come to our school there will be lots of people just like you and you will have lots of friends just like you do here" (1 year post project).

An ongoing project

Once visits start (once a week for an hour), the school and kindergarten buddies have the same story of their previous visit experience to put in their respective portfolios, which they do together. This is the first interaction of the weekly visit, and often the children spend time reviewing the previous stories, talking about what happened and what they did together. This is a good settling in period and gives them a chance to work together one on one. After this has been completed, the buddies go out into the kindergarten environment and play together, enjoying activities like constructing with hot melt glue guns, climbing, and working in the sandpit or the art area.

When am I going to get a buddy?

Once the initial group of school buddies started visiting kindergarten, we began to get interest from parents of children who transition to the other local school and from the children themselves. On a buddy visit day, one child who knew he was coming up to 5 years old said very forcefully, "When am I going to get a buddy?" The teacher explained to him that he was not going to go to the school where the buddies came from and we had only just begun talking about extending this programme to his future school. He was not to be convinced that this was a good enough reason for him not to have a buddy, so the teacher suggested he might like to write to the school deputy principal and the teacher would scan and email his request. Ben very quickly drew himself and wrote his name, and then when the teacher thought out loud that she might need to write, "Can I have a buddy please", he responded instantly with, "I can do that" and very confidently wrote a message using his own script! His letter was dispatched by email and a very positive reply came almost immediately that after the holidays he would have a buddy. "Yeah", he said, "I've got a buddy", which prompted five other children to write (with Ben showing how it was done) at once and

DEAR BEN

THANK YOU SO MUCH FOR YOUR GREAT PICTURE-IT WAS REALLY COOL TO HEAR FROM YOU.

YES BEN, YOU WILL HAVE A BUDDY WHEN YOU START SCHOOL. YOU WILL MEET YOUR BUDDY AFTER THE HOLIDAYS.

WE ARE REALLY LOOKING FORWARD TO YOU VISITING OUR SCHOOL AND KNOW THAT YOU WILL MAKE LOTS OF NEW FRIENDS HERE.

COME AND SAY HELLO TO ME THE NEXT TIME YOU ARE HERE WITH YOUR MUM

receiving the same affirmative answer. These school buddy children are Year 4 students, and they come for an hour a week on a different day to the first school buddy group.

Impact of the buddies project

Now we work with both schools on the buddies project and each has had unexpected impacts, both within the kindergarten and beyond. The positive effects of the relationship building have so far had a wide influence. At both schools older children accost the teacher involved in the project, putting their case to be a buddy. It is seen as a prestigious position within each school and is most sought after. Recently parents have been known to put the case for their child to be able to be a school buddy (often informally, at the school road crossing or in the playground after school).

Parents or caregivers who meet the school buddy on the first enrolment interview with the school have reported on the outstanding job the buddies do as role models. The school buddy takes responsibility for showing them around the school and promotes the school as a place of enjoyment and learning. This was particularly evident for one child, who was very reluctant about moving to school and also adamant that she did not need to go to school "because I can read and write already". After one session with her school buddy she reported to her mother, "I'm going to Rosie's school!" (Conversation with parent, project year 3). Her mother later wrote in her portfolio:

> What a delightful young girl Rosie is!! CJ is certainly a fan as well. On the morning of her interview at the school the office lady commented on seeing CJ running into the school with such excitement. She was looking forward to seeing her buddy again … thanks to the FANTASTIC teachers the school and kindergarten I'm confident that her transition to school will be a doddle (for CJ that is. Her Mum on the other hand may require a lot more support!) (Project year 3).

Later, in a focus interview, the same parent reported of her daughter, "what she wants to be when she grows up is a buddy", and another parent followed by saying "they all do".

The school buddies are seen by the kindergarten children as familiar in a strange new place, and after meeting her buddy on a 'prior to school' visit and building an enduring friendship during kindergarten visits, Charlotte's mum commented, "I think she wasn't sure about coming to school ... she was so settled at kindy, she just didn't want it to end and Hannah was the only link from getting her out of kindy into school". Charlotte was so taken with her buddy, Hannah, that Hannah became the first person on Charlotte's fifth birthday party list (and she attended the party).

The cross school relationship

Interestingly for us, there have been other unexpected outcomes from the buddies project within the school environment. This was demonstrated when a parent commented on the relationships her son had formed with children in the senior school:

> I did see him quite often with older kids and I would say 'Who are they?' And he'd say 'That's so and so's buddy, and that's so and so'... there's actually a few that he knows". (Parent focus group, 1 year post project).

She was surprised and delighted to see her new entrant child making friends among the senior school and felt that he would be well taken care of because of these friendships. Within this parent group it was reported on several occasions that "it gives them empathy towards younger kids". A teacher reported that the division between senior school and junior school had been considerably diminished, to the extent that, to his surprise, he had "littlies" visiting his classroom of their own accord to find their big buddies.

Another parent remarked that her child:

> is normally a shy little boy ... you know real passive ... and having Jordan as a buddy strengthened him and every time I was around I always saw Jordan ... if I just drove past at lunchtime ... and I'd just park my car over there and I'd just go over ... and Jordan was playing with him (Parent focus group, 1 year post project).

She felt the buddy relationship had strengthened her child and given her child confidence in the new setting, and she was "very grateful and thankful there's such a thing as a buddy". The cumulative effect of the buddy friendships was noted as well:

> cos they make friends with buddies' friends as well ... I think Oscar's made friends with some of the other older kids and I'm always amazed when we walk through the school, how many of the older kids say 'hello Oscar'. (Parent focus group, 1 year post project)

This cumulative effect led to a further consequence in the second year after the end of the project in this school, when the school teachers came to an agreement to reassign classrooms, and now the school pattern is a senior classroom next to a junior classroom all along the corridors. This was seen as having developed out of the buddies project, which built connections between the senior school and the junior school.

Another school-initiated development included 'lead buddies', where a child is designated as the leader of the school buddies and takes responsibility for communication and organisation. This school is organising for children to apply to be a buddy, and to take part in an interview where they can put forward their relevant qualities that show their suitability to be a buddy. Both schools have also reorganised senior timetables to allow school buddies more time with their new entrant buddy.

Concluding comments

In New Zealand, both curriculum documents, *The New Zealand Curriculum* and *Te Whāriki* contain curriculum statements that have goals advocating building on previous learning in each setting. The deliberate direct link between learning dispositions, key competencies and the working theories of the two curricula creates opportunities for continuity of learning experience (Carr, 2006). It is important that transition practices are consistently and coherently built on this notion of children developing competence, accessing resources and building relationships.

It is clear that a buddy/mentor relationship between a child in the early childhood centre and an older school child is an example of a tuakana/teina relationship that supports the younger child to learn about school and building competence. The relationship can empower the new entrant in their new role as a school pupil. It supports continuity by providing knowledge and information from an older, more experienced person within the school system. However, Brooker (2008) reminds us that "reciprocity takes time to become established" (p. 102), and this could impact on the effectiveness of this approach as a transition tool. Building a friendship is normally a process that occurs over an extended period of time, and we have seen that developing a tuakana/teina relationship to support transition for a preschool child needs an investment of time in an environment that supports the development of friendships.

CHAPTER 7

Theory building

In addition to supporting transition to school, our aim in developing the various projects had been to foster relationships between the teachers in the early childhood and primary school sectors. However, as these projects progressed it became clear that many other participants were involved, and so we began to discuss ways in which we could locate this developing network within a theoretical framework. A feature of action research is that data are accumulated and analysed concurrently (Cardno, 2003; Mutch, 2005). This formative approach to data analysis enabled us to get a sense of how a project or resource development was proceeding, and to determine the best way forward. As a result, we accumulated a considerable amount of data, and although we were able to see some themes emerging, we were conscious of the need to conceptually organise these findings in some way.

Action project designs are often described in terms of a spiral of self-reflective cycles or steps. One of the criteria of success for these cycles is whether participants have developed a stronger and more authentic sense of understanding and development in their practice and the situations in which they practise (Kemmis & McTaggart, 2000, p. 595). Many teachers teach intuitively, and an opportunity to reflect on their implicit practices can be enlightening and helpful. However, practitioner research, in collaboration with university researchers, also has the capacity to construct theory and to contribute to an understanding of knowing and learning that goes beyond the local. We agree with the view that "practitioners are among those who have the authority to construct Knowledge (with a capital K) about teaching and learning" (Cochran-Smith & Donnell, 2006, p. 508).

One way in which we reflected on our research and made sense of the data we were accumulating through joint projects with schools was to construct theory by devising diagrams. In order to conceptualise the involvement of multiple parties in the development and use of resources that crossed the educational borders, the research team devised a diagram of a framework that summarised the analysis (Figure 1).

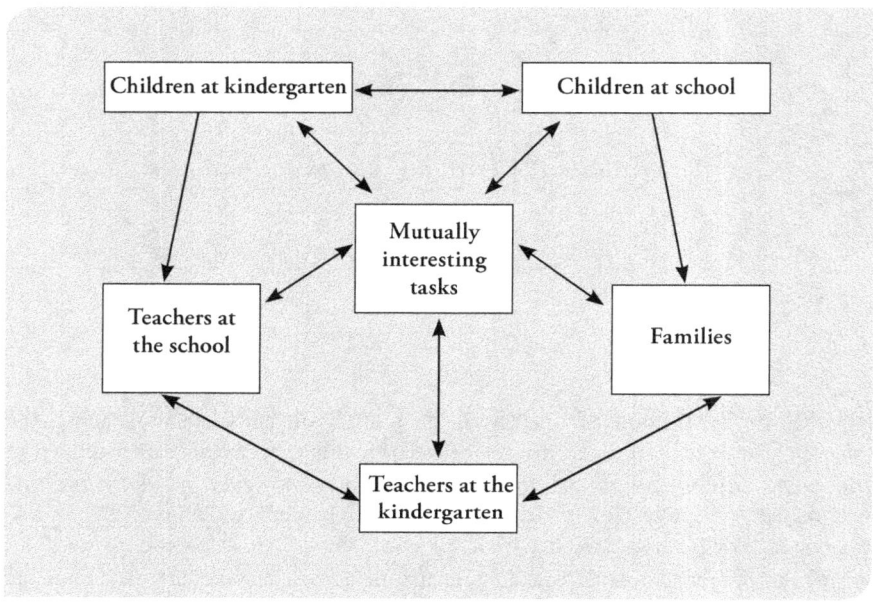

FIGURE 1: FRAMEWORK FOR ANALYSING JOINT PROJECTS

The framework was applied to each project as it was developed, and we used the term "mutually interesting tasks" at the centre to represent each of the collaborative projects. Initially, the arrows went from the centre box out to the five groups of participants, to indicate that interactions and relationships were built *through* the project. However, as our understanding, interpretation and application of the framework developed, we realised that the connections were being forged *between* the groups as well as to the central task or project. As a result, double-headed arrows were added around the outside to indicate the flow between each of the participants, and to emphasise the new relationships that were developing (for example, the relationships the children at school were forming with the children and teachers at kindergarten). Applying the analysis framework to each new resource in this way meant we were able to evaluate the resource in relation to each particular stakeholder in the group, as well as through the lens of each of our three research questions.

We found that this framework enabled us to clearly analyse each mutually interesting project and determine the different people involved, and it also helped us to reflect on what made projects effective and successful. Some of the collaborative projects involved all of the groups of participants, while some involved only a few at any one time. A pattern began to emerge, indicating that the most successful projects were those that involved more of the participants. There was also evidence to show that the degree to which the projects were mutually interesting was important. For example, the *Welcome to School* DVD (explained in detail in Chapter 4) included all five groups of participants and was of interest to everyone. Throughout the course of the research, this data analysis framework helped us to make sense of the data we were gathering.

Retrospective data analysis and theorising

However, when we came to revisit the analysis of our data and report our journey for the purpose of writing this book, we came to see that this early framework, while initially very helpful in grounding our thinking and giving us a clear picture of each individual project and who was involved, was very static. We felt that it did not adequately represent the developing relationships between the different participants and how they are drawn together over time through the projects. We were conscious of the sociocultural and ecological nature of our journey and the fact that it was unique to our context, but we were also committed to providing a useful framework for others to apply to their own setting in order to make use of what we had learned.

Development over time was an important factor for the researchers, enabling a retrospective look at how projects had evolved and the developments that were made. We were striving for a framework that, at a glance, would indicate some of the complexities and important aspects of each individual project. In reflecting back over the data gathered, and after gathering more recent data, we envisaged a framework that showed how each project progressed, including who initiated the project, when groups of participants became involved, how all the participants worked together and how the projects gathered momentum over time. In light of this, and after much discussion and deliberation, the research team developed a new conceptual framework (Figure 2) to represent our journey with each project, and to show how the development and use of each project were influenced by the important and influential aspects of time, movement, growth and momentum.

We felt it was important to demonstrate the impact of time on both the relationships and the projects. The successful projects achieved their goal of supporting the transition to school quite quickly, but over time, as more participants became involved and their influence was woven into the project, the value of the project in building a bridge between people and settings was realised. The momentum of those already on board with the project helped to carry it forward, and as it progressed it drew in other strategic participants. There was a cumulative effect over time as well, with engagement from key players occurring more quickly with subsequent projects.

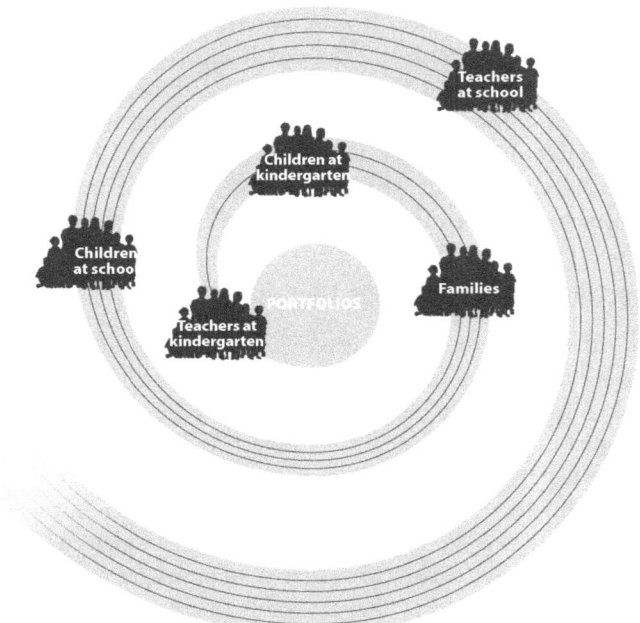

FIGURE 2: REVISED FRAMEWORK FOR ANALYSING JOINT PROJECTS:
THE PORTFOLIOS

(Diagrams drawn by Aaron Smith)

Figure 2 takes the form of a koru spiral, with the mutually interesting project in the centre. The initiating participants are close to the centre, at the start of the project, and as the spiral unfurls more and more participants are drawn in and become involved. The participants are drawn in at different places on the spiral, indicating when they became involved in the project, with the main participants closer to the centre of the koru. In this way the framework indicates movement, as there is a place for participating groups to be placed closer together or further away, indicating the time participants took to come on board with each project.

We felt that using the koru spiral gave the framework significant meaning for us in a New Zealand context. In New Zealand the koru is an image that is inspired by the young unfurling frond of the ponga (a tree fern endemic to New Zealand) and symbolises new life, growth and strength. The unfurling fronds open up numerous possibilities, much like the multilateral relationships that were emerging through the projects. Like the koru spiral, the new framework illustrates the origin of the project at the centre, while representing the movement and growth forward and out.

Another productive use of the analysis framework diagram was to identify projects that had only a limited influence. If projects were not mutually interesting across the broad range of participants, there was minimal engagement and, as a result, little growth in the project. An example of this is the school photo display board. It was useful to start conversations between children, families and kindergarten teachers about the imminent move to school, but the school was not engaged with this process. It was not until much later, when the school became involved through the buddy project, asking for photos of the schoolchildren with their kindergarten buddies to display in the school classroom, that the connections between a wider range of settings and participants increased the significance of this transition artifact. Once again, it is only over time that this progress has been realised.

Once the project is initiated, the journey is represented on the framework with a line, which continues around the spiral until the next group of participants is drawn in. Each time this happens, another line starts and runs around the spiral alongside the other lines. This shows how, after becoming involved in the project, the participants move forwards on the project journey together, working collaboratively alongside each other as the spiral grows and the project journey gains momentum. We found that we could also apply the framework retrospectively, and place portfolios (our first mutually interesting project) at the centre of the framework. The level of involvement by the participants confirmed our interpretation of portfolios as a valuable artifact for transition. Initially, all of the mutually interesting projects began with the kindergarten teachers initiating the interactions, and in many of the earlier projects it took some time to draw in others. Our belief in the importance of the projects sustained us, as did our belief that as early childhood teachers who value perseverance and resilience in children we needed to promote these dispositions in our work. The time it took for some of the projects to get underway gave us the opportunity to reflect deeply, and to articulate in a heartfelt way the importance of the projects in supporting the children and their families in the transition to school.

We were aware from previous research of the kinds of outcomes that are possible from establishing strong relationships and working together (Brostrom, 2002, 2007; Dockett & Perry, 1999, 2001, 2002, 2003, 2005; Einarsdottir, 2006; Margetts, 2002, 2007; Peters, 2002, 2003, 2004), and this encouraged us and gave us the impetus to maintain our vision and enthusiasm in the face of challenges. As we worked together, and the relationships became stronger, the time it took for others to become engaged was reduced and the participants moved closer to the start of the project—often right at the start of the journey. In this way we moved away from the kindergarten teachers always taking the lead, to beginning projects with participants side by side. Analysing the projects over time with the new framework afforded us the opportunity to show how the relationships between all of the key players have changed and developed.

This progress was apparent in the later stages of the research project, when the buddy project was initiated. The idea came from a parent and was picked

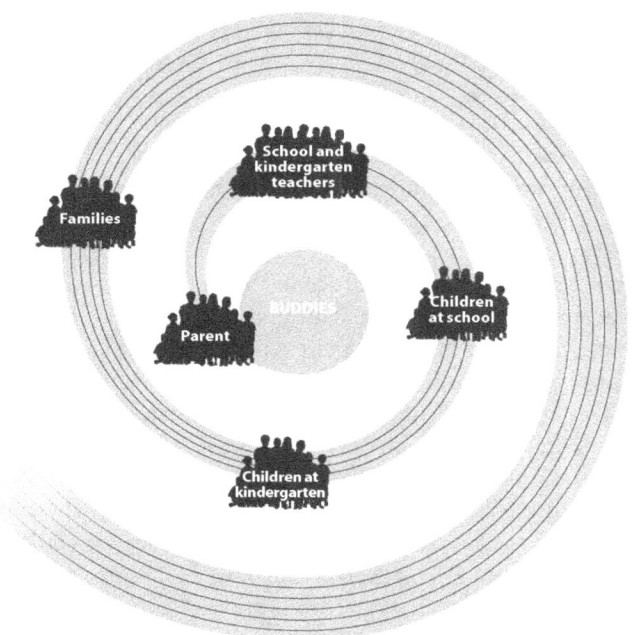

FIGURE 3: FRAMEWORK FOR ANALYSING JOINT PROJECTS: BUDDIES

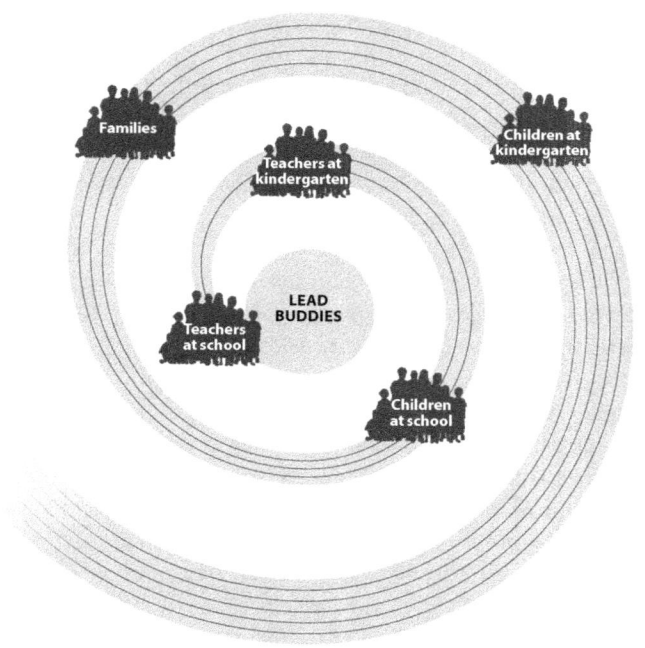

FIGURE 4: FRAMEWORK FOR ANALYSING JOINT PROJECTS: LEAD BUDDIES

up by the kindergarten and then the school in quick succession. In an extension of the buddy project, in the second year after the research both schools were discussing the initiation of new projects with the kindergarten and taking responsibility for getting them started. One example is the lead buddy project, described in Chapter 6. At an informal meeting between the teachers of the kindergarten and the school to discuss progress, the school teachers proposed the idea of having lead buddies. The school teachers were looking at ways they could draw on the experience of the children who had already been buddies and add to the development of their leadership skills. Lead buddies attend the initial new buddy meeting and liaise between all partners in this initiative.

The use of the framework to analyse data from each project showed quite clearly that as we progressed with our relationships over subsequent projects, the groups of participants moved closer and closer together, showing that with an established relationship, collaboration came about more quickly and we undertook more projects alongside each other from the beginning.

As each project evolved, and we experienced the benefits of forging stronger and deeper relationships with children, families and teachers at school, it was clear to us that the work we were doing was benefiting the children, the families and the schools in the transition process. What we learned with each project not only strengthened our relationships but also added to our fund of knowledge of what was required in order for a "mutually interesting project" to be successful, starting with smaller projects and building on these as the relationship grows and becomes more established. The analysis framework supported our thinking by allowing us to describe and explain what we were trying to achieve, and we were able to use it to evaluate the projects as they progressed. The circular nature of the new analysis framework also represents the cyclical nature of action research, whereby revisiting the journey is an accepted part of the process. Evaluation and analysis inevitably take into account prior endeavours, and even with several projects underway at the same time there is constant appraisal and review of developments.

Different projects are mutually interesting to different people, and some are more successful than others, but we found that more important than the project itself and the valuable transition artifacts produced were the relationships that were formed and built on while working on a project together.

Reciprocal relationships across sectors

As the research progressed it became clear that there was good will from both the early childhood and primary sectors to foster strong cross-sector relationships, but that there were a number of issues that could affect this. First, relationships take time to develop. This project built on a long history of Mangere Bridge Kindergarten working together with one school, while the contact with the second school developed throughout the 3 years of the research. Staff changes in all settings mean that these relationships are constantly renegotiated. Persistence and enthusiasm seem to be important qualities for teachers in both sectors as we seek to maintain or develop relationships that support children's transitions.

The issues of reciprocity and power are other important considerations. Although someone has to take the initiative and make the first contact, in an ongoing relationship ideally teachers hoped for "an equal partnership, it's not all coming and being pushed by, from the kindy or pushed and pulled by the school" (Teacher D, interview, project year 3). Teachers hoped for opportunities to "make some input" and to take turns to host meetings and raise their concerns and suggestions (Teacher A, interview, project year 3), and that both sides would listen to each other and have "a two-way" discussion (Teacher F, interview, project year 3), so that misunderstandings did not arise, leading to individuals feeling frustrated and their voices not being heard or valued:

> I don't want to see this as a school thing thinking up things … and telling the kindy. I think the conversations need to keep happening between the kindy teachers and the school teachers. This is going really well, what else could we do? How else could this progress? (Teacher E, interview, project year 3)

Having the opportunity to visit the kindergarten was valued by many of the school teachers, who were impressed by what they saw:

> Let's go up to the kindergarten and see some of the independence that the children are using and let's use that and continue that here because I think that some of the things that the children are doing independently up there get lost when they come to school. (Teacher F, interview, project year 3)

All teachers are busy, and clarity regarding the specific purpose and possible outcomes of meetings, and, where possible, avoiding cancellations, helped to avoid confusion and disappointment. In addition, although key figures in each setting helped to establish the contacts, sharing responsibilities was also helpful:

> My concern at the moment is it started with me as the new entrant teacher. My focus now is making sure each new entrant teacher that comes in after that actually has all of that knowledge and I don't think they do at the moment … It's just something that has become part of what we do and new teachers, it's just an expectation that we'll carry on. (Teacher D, interview, project year 3)

By the end of the project there was considerable satisfaction expressed by the school teachers:

> I really like the relationship we've got with them [Mangere Bridge Kindergarten teachers] and that's a really positive thing … the relationship is so important and just the way they've included us in everything. (Teacher B, interview, project year 3)

> So now it's all set up it's working out ways to maintain it as it is now … and also thinking about new ways to strengthen the relationships. (Teacher D, interview, project year 3)

> Well I've been involved in it for a long time and I think it's absolutely wonderful. I think we're very lucky here to be involved with a preschool

> that's a Centre of Innovation and we have very close links with the staff at the preschool there for the benefit of the families and the children involved … There are no issues, absolutely no issues with them and we hope that they're really happy with us and we just want to continue from where they start with a child. (Teacher G, interview, project year 3)

Having a good relationship with Mangere Bridge Kindergarten also led some teachers to want to foster this with other ECE services that fed into their schools:

> I think it's just the relationship we need to build up like the relationship we've got with Mangere Bridge … to have that sort of relationship with all the ones that send the children here would be really good … I think it's just a matter of somebody approaching them and saying 'now look, we've had some children from your kindy, can we work together if you know they're coming to us'. (Teacher B, interview, project year 3)

Concluding comments

Transition to school is a process that involves three distinct settings: the home, the kindergarten and the school. In an effort to analyse the effectiveness of each mutually interesting project we collaborated on we devised a framework that clarified for us what was important for the projects to be successful. Our analysis showed that the projects that were most successful were those that drew in the greatest number of participants. Not only did that mean that more interested parties had input into the development of the project, but it also created more opportunities for relationships to be established and strengthened across all sectors and between all key players. A level of trust and collaboration was built over time, providing a strong foundation for future projects.

One of the key aspects that we found strongly influenced progress was that the projects needed willing players—participants who wanted to be engaged in projects that were mutually interesting. All the key participants also needed to demonstrate a degree of flexibility in order to work together for the best possible outcomes of the project. Projects needed to be able to be sustained over time, although they did require review from time to time to gauge their effectiveness in the new and emerging relationships that were developing.

At the outset, the kindergarten teachers were aware that the responsibility lay with them to make the first move and initiate projects, and their willingness to do so signalled their commitment to both the families and the schools. What was found to be key in establishing the first connections was developing an idea the participants were willing to collaborate on, and in some instances this took time. The emergent structure of this process reflects Wenger's idea of learning in a community of practice, and how new practice comes out of the negotiation of meaning (Wenger, 1998). Although we were working collaboratively with the essential groups involved in making transition to school successful, how we got there required consultation, dialogue, understanding and agreement.

The data analysis spiral is designed to indicate that there is no fixed end point for each individual project. Each one is open to a number of possibilities—to run its course to a point where the artifact or supporting practice is no longer required, to lead on to other new project, or to cycle back and be re-formed in a new way or for a new purpose. As relationships develop and change, new pathways emerge to take the journey in a new direction.

CHAPTER 8

Multi-literacies that support the crossing of borders

Literacy is an especially valued domain of expertise. It is valued by teachers in all educational sectors, by families, and in educational policies in New Zealand and across the world. We do not share the view that literacy education begins at school, and we have sought ways to conceptualise literacy as a curriculum area that crosses the boundary between the kindergarten and school. Children tend to "learn to read" at school, but they learn to become literate in multiple ways from a very early age. This chapter focuses on children's learning through multiple literacy practices in the kindergarten, and on how these practices support literacy transitions for children and their families. Transition to school is based on the analogy of crossing a border from one place to another and one set of languages to another. These two border crossings are very closely related: strengthening children's communication skills and dispositions strengthens their learning across multiple borders (including into school).

Although the experiences of children with English as an additional language are woven throughout the book, this chapter includes specific discussion of strengthening languages and literacies for this group. Using case studies, the stories of participation in multi-literacy events for the children are seen as defining children's view of themselves as capable and competent literacy learners who use and create a variety of literacy tools—photos, film, written and oral texts and environmental images such as McDonalds' golden arches etc.

Multi-literacies

The New London Group (2000) gives two reasons for broadening the definition of literacy in today's world.
* Communities have increasingly diverse cultural and linguistic backgrounds (this is certainly so in this kindergarten and in the local and wider community).

- Emerging digital technologies have influenced the way societies communicate and interact.

To enable children and families to participate fully in the community of the kindergarten, we suggest that the use of multi-literacies, as defined by Unsworth (2001), should be an integral part of the ideas and planning around literacy. Unsworth explains that by the time children begin school they have been exposed to a diverse range of multi-modal text experiences, through signs, visual images (even on children's clothing), computers, film, television and games, as well as written text. Although digital images and computer text are commonly used, they have not replaced conventional literacy practices but instead now complement them.

Our kindergarten is culturally and linguistically diverse, and the function of language suggested by Freire, "to read the word and the world" (cited in Lankshear & Knobel, 2003, p. 5), captures the philosophy of a dynamic integrated approach to literacy pedagogical practices within our programme. Literacy at Mangere Bridge Kindergarten is understood to be a holistic, complex and dynamic process, which develops differently for each individual child. It is seen as highly contextual, and as a social and cultural construct (Gee, 2008; Lankshear, & Knobel, 2003; Makin et al. 2007).

Moviemaking

In order to acknowledge the different strengths that children bring to the literacy mix, and to expand on children's prior knowledge and experience, digital stories were created that linked their home and cultural experiences to those in the kindergarten and provided opportunities for children to work together in a community of learners. In our experience, the making of movies using children's own stories contributes to complexity of thinking, to meeting their minds, and to them working together to understand and use the visual image to interpret thinking. This is an important foundation for future learning. As Brostrom (2005) suggests:

> transition to formal education entails crossing boundaries from the activity system of play to the activity system of school learning, so leading to the development of learning motive. To facilitate children's transition to school preschool teachers should provide activities which influence the development of children's motivation to learn. (p. 17)

In her work with young school-aged children, Vivien Gussin Paley reminds us of the connection between play and cognitive thinking when she says, "It was when I asked the children to dictate their stories and bring them to life again on a stage that the connections between play and analytical thinking became clear" (Paley, 2004, p.11–12). Moviemaking constitutes a multi-modal literacy practice, not focused only on printed text but enabling the telling of the stories and the reading of the world through visual images.

Creating movie scripts by drawing a picture and orally telling the story to the teacher, who then writes it down, was the format used for beginning movie scripts in the research. Using those scripts and then acting them out acknowledged the diverse literacy practices in this community. Like the majority of children in the ECE community in New Zealand, our children are exposed to television programmes, video games, toys, video and digital cameras, and computer use in the home. Often their scripts strongly reflect the influence of mass media culture—superheroes in all their forms, or dragons and knights and princesses. The resulting literacy artifact, a DVD of the story, can then be revisited time and time again and is valued by the child.

On each occasion, at the outset of the moviemaking experience the teacher asked the child to draw a picture/plan and then write the story down. The child/scriptwriter then needed to find actors, decide on props, create the props if necessary, decide on a location and direct the camera person. During the filming episodes, different children played their part as an actor in the production of the movie but also became learner scriptwriters, prop makers and directors themselves, and would carefully watch the process and become the next child to want to produce a movie.

Many of the stories had similar storylines, and several knight and dragon movies were made over a short time. Included in the moviemaking were several children for whom English was an additional language. In one instance the star of a segment of one of the early movies was a Middle Eastern child who had watched the previous movies and inserted herself into the production by getting out the tea-set and serving the "princesses" who were being filmed—and who were about to be chased by the dragons. This was a familiar activity, as she often played "Mums and Dads" in the family/dough area. As a home event and a familiar kindergarten event, this became a familiar task that provided an 'in' to being an actor in the production, even though for this child English was a language she had had very little exposure to.

On a separate occasion, another child acted and scripted a variation to the script. While the princesses were happily dancing and twirling, this child, for whom English was an additional language, acted as the dog, barking from the sidelines. The variation was accepted by the main scriptwriter for this movie and was included in the emerging script, which is highly indicative of the inclusiveness of the moviemaking process.

Once the movies were burned to a DVD this literacy artifact, produced by the children and the teachers together, became a resource that was not restrictive, or dependent on being able to read the English language, but inclusive in that it could be enjoyed by a wide audience of diverse families with diverse language backgrounds in the home. The DVD can also fulfil the function of providing the family—especially parents of children for whom English is an additional language—with a picture of their child participating in a literacy event, belonging to the group, and enjoying the activity. In the feedback and stories from parents, this aspect of the moviemaking figured largely as a bonus.

Nicholas' story: a leader emerges

Nicholas, a bilingual Tongan and English speaker, had over his time at kindergarten been through several periods when he had been quite unsettled first thing in the morning. He had difficulty letting his aunt or grandmother go until a teacher engaged him in an activity that involved supporting him to find someone to play with. One day he began beatboxing while playing with a couple of boys during a morning session and then taught other children how to beatbox. Over the next few days we recorded the beatboxing onto GarageBand (a software package developed by Apple that allows users to create music) and then burned it to a CD, which Nicholas took home. It was accompanied by the learning story in his portfolio.

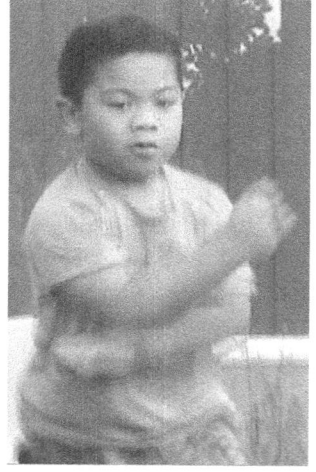

Next Nicholas began to show other children how to hiphop dance, and he joined a movie being made by another child called the *Kindergarten Dance Party*. Nicholas and two other boys asked if they could hiphop on the movie, and they expertly and enthusiastically jumped, rolled and waved hiphop arm movements, dancing in time with the hiphop CD. Over the time of making the beatboxing CD and then the *Dance Party* movie, Nicholas' confidence grew daily and he came in each day ready, willing and able to join in with the group of hiphop and superhero boys. There was also a marked change in the way he engaged with other children and adults.

In conversation with his mother a week later, she recounted how Nicholas had watched the DVD many times—more than 20—and that he insisted on watching it every morning before kindergarten. She was unaware of his interest in beatboxing and hiphop, and was surprised at his technical expertise in this area.

Nicholas' motivation to become involved emerged through his interest in beatboxing and hiphopping, and his self-assurance as leader and learner was captured on the DVD, which he returned to over and over. He became a pivotal member of the dance group, a leader and an expert at dance and music.

By participating in a multi-modal literacy event using body expression, and by contributing to a recorded interpretation of the dance leading other children in moves to the music, Nicholas was participating in a group action that became part of the cultural practice of the kindergarten. His participation in this collective event set him up in his portfolio as the expert at some things the school may value—dancing and being a leader. Both the portfolio story and the DVD provide for a negotiation of his status as a learner in a new setting. Through his participation in a shared experience, and in a creative literacy event, Nicholas' agency was acknowledged positively as a valuable learning experience, and his leadership skills were recognised.

Pharoah's story: a perfect dragon death

Pharoah, a child for whom English is an additional language, spent a large proportion of his time at kindergarten outside, involved in superhero scripted dramatic play. His play was largely non-verbal and very energetic. When the moviemaking began, Pharoah took an intense interest and was a bit player in several movies. However, when the knight movie was filmed once again and a dragon was needed, Pharoah showed his willingness to be one of the dragon actors by running off to get a costume and arriving ready to take part. At the crucial moment in the movie, when the dragons were to lie down and die, the two other dragons were very reluctant, but Pharoah knew exactly what was required and crumpled to the ground, closed his eyes and stayed slumped, a dead dragon indeed.

Pharoah's story offers another example of participation in collectively produced and shared activities:

> Crucial to the nature of membership is participation in collective activities that signify that one is part of a group and collective action. At the same time, cultural practices in these routines prepare, or prime, members for future transitions. (Corsaro & Molinari, 2005, p. 17)

Pharoah later took part in several superhero movies with this group of children, who had built a relationship during superhero play. Pharoah's dramatic experiences provided opportunities for him to communicate and build relationships.

Alice's story: a tale of a doggy adventure.

Alice's dog movie was actually instigated by Corryn, who had watched the making of several knight/superhero movies and wanted to be a princess in a movie. Alice came along and had some ideas for a story and she helped put together the script. Moviemaking had taken on a life of its own by this time at our kindergarten, and Corryn first, and then Alice, knew exactly what to do. They agreed on a story, went off to find actors and get them dressed in costume, and then came to tell the teacher who was the camera person that they were ready to film. This filming effort took just a morning, and then we edited the movie by working together to add titles, sound and special effects.

Although Corryn initiated this project, she was quite happy to work with Alice to get the movie underway. It was a collaborative effort and included children who had not previously taken part in filming a movie. The movie script involved the dog moving across the playground and up into the 'castle', and consequently the concept of movie animation was introduced to the actors in this learning event.

The change of focus from knights and dragons to the dog movie was a huge success. After watching Alice's dog movie, James' sister commented, "Mum tell him to stop we've watched it eight times this morning." James was in charge of the remote, and before kindergarten he kept playing and playing the movie, in which he starred as a dragon.

Portfolios as multi-faceted documentation of learning

Movies on DVD are added to the children's portfolios. The portfolios fulfil a multi-faceted role within the kindergarten: as assessment tools, as tools of engagement (as explained in Chapter 3) and, most importantly for the analysis in this chapter, as literacy tools that are useful for documenting children's literacy practices and for drawing in family literacy practices. McNaughton's (2001) research highlights the crucial importance of connecting literacy practices in the children's home and educational settings. Consequently, the portfolio role within the kindergarten is not singular or one-dimensional. The portfolios are a multi-faceted documentation of learning using ICT (digital photos and stories, movies on DVD, music CDs), all of which have proven invaluable in the process of engaging families in the literacy practices within the kindergarten.

Providing a range of ICT at the kindergarten has supported the engagement of all participants in the development of further resources across the transition border (see Chapters 4 and 5). As Healey (2008) notes:

> it is crucial that teachers acknowledge that these digital access points are a reality for many children, who learn as much about their world, language, and literacies by selecting and designing how and what they view and do, as from the people around them. (p. 6)

Within the portfolios are narratives that can be read by the children and families. These narratives present opportunities for acknowledging the learning that occurs for children in the home and community, as well as within the educational setting. The narratives include those that relate to the children's movies on DVD that can be viewed at home by the family.

Parents' feedback about the movie was extremely enthusiastic

Nicole's mum wrote in her daughter's kindergarten portfolio:

> We were all very excited about Paul's Knight movie and getting to see all the children participating in the movie. Our family sat down to watch the movie and were very excited to see Nicole being a dragon. She often wants to be a dragon when she plays at kindy, so it was nice to see her being a dragon in the movie & participating & having fun. We were so proud of her & loved watching the movie & showing it to her grandparents & uncle/aunty. We can't wait to see the next movie—thank you Mangere Bridge kindergarten for a special movie experience. (Project year 1)

And a father wrote similarly in his son's portfolio:

> Ethyn comes home excited about his superhero play with friends at kindy. He speaks with confidence and has so much energy that sometimes we have to tell him to slow down. To see this much enjoyment in him makes me as a parent feel good that he is enjoying socialising and interacting with other classmates. It is an awesome experience watching Ethyn grow with confidence. Keep up the hard work. (Project year 1).

Concluding comments

Healy's view of the world as an increasingly diverse literacy landscape that requires teachers to adopt a different approach to literacy aligns with our beliefs about holistic inclusive practices that "meet the minds" of the children:

> Where print literacies privileged some learners over others, multimodal literacies enable a more open architecture in which to learn and the conversion of the passive print classroom audience into active cultural participants. (Healy, 2008, p. xiii)

This aligns with the notion of teachers and children learning together using multi-modal literacies in an environment where children can access the resources, and design and produce their own learning path across the transition border.

There is no doubt that children who have developed authoring capabilities and experiences before they go to school can be expected to be alert to creative literacy opportunities in other places. These opportunities must be made available, yet most primary schools in the Western world focus their literacy programmes in the first year of school on decoding print text and writing. We have not so far been able to connect the moviemaking experiences of the 3 and 4 year olds to the literacy programme in the first 2 years of school, other than by using the very common practice of asking children to draw a picture and write a caption underneath. In our view, the potential is there to use moviemaking as a context for developing a love of story, a recognition of what makes a good story, and the planning of a logical and sequential script. Perhaps that is our next border-crossing challenge.

CHAPTER 9

Building bridges: The alignment between an early childhood and a school curriculum

This chapter looks closely at one of the children's portfolios from Mangere Bridge Kindergarten in order to focus on specific aspects of border crossing. In this case the crossing is between an early childhood curriculum and the school curriculum of the contributing schools, and we analyse the learning stories in one early childhood portfolio through the lens of five *key competencies* set out as mandatory outcomes in the school curriculum. In a sense it is a uniquely New Zealand story because of the way in which, since 2007, dispositional outcomes in the texts of both curriculum documents have been aligned. But we also see it as a curriculum-in-action alignment: enacted dispositional outcomes from early childhood learning environments to school. And therefore this alignment is about the continuity of learning across educational sector borders (early childhood, primary, secondary and tertiary) for any nation in which aspirations for school graduates includes such qualities as connected, actively involved citizens and confident life-long learners (Ministry of Education, 2007 p.8).

At the end of the second year of the Centre of Innovation project a new school curriculum document was published. What was notable about this document was the addition of "key competencies" as outcomes, including a diagram (Ministry of Education, 2007 p. 42) of the cross-sector alignment between *Te Whāriki* and *The New Zealand Curriculum*, and on into tertiary education, see Table 9.1 for an adapted version.

The New Zealand early childhood curriculum: Te Whāriki	The New Zealand (school) Curriculum	Tertiary
Exploration →	Thinking →	Thinking
Communication →	Using language, symbols & text →	Using tools interactively
Well-being →	Managing self →	Acting autonomously
Contribution →	Relating to others →	Operating in social groups
Belonging →	Participating and contributing →	

TABLE 9.1: A CROSS-SECTOR PATHWAY
Source: Ministry of Education, 2007, p. 42

In the diagram, all these sector frameworks are connected by arrows, describing continuities of curriculum pathways and learning journeys. This was an exciting development for education in New Zealand. It clearly sign-posted a learning pathway from early childhood to school, one that was consistent with *Te Whāriki* strands and learning dispositions and was not defined entirely in terms of subject-based knowledge and skill, and the bridge between early childhood and school was not only paved with literacy and numeracy markers. The research team for the Mangere Bridge Centre of Innovation had been involved in the early work for this new school curriculum. Both of the research associates had been on a curriculum development advisory group, and in 2006 Carol participated in a local school's preparation of feedback on the 2006 draft. She contributed papers from the research associates and took part in discussions.

Outcomes in the early childhood curriculum are described as working theories and learning dispositions, and an inspection of the texts of the two curriculum documents (see Carr, et al., 2008), together with the literature on key competencies from their original source, the OECD (see Rychen & Salganik, 2001, 2003), affirms the alignment between the two curriculum documents. The early childhood curriculum states that 'knowledge, skills and attitudes are closely linked (p.44); key competencies in the school curriculum (p. 42) are described as "more complex than skills"; they "draw also on knowledge, attitudes, and values in ways that lead to action" (p.12). The early childhood curriculum states that "Children learn through responsive and reciprocal relationships with people, places, and things" (p. 43); the school curriculum states that key competencies "continue to develop over time, shaped by interactions with people, places, ideas, and things" (p. 12). The school curriculum further comments that:

> Opportunities to develop the competencies occur in social contexts. People adopt and adapt practices that they see used and valued by those closest to them, and they make these practices part of their own identity and expertise. (p. 12)

A child's portfolio

This chapter was inspired by this new alignment. We interrogated a case study child's portfolio to explore the following questions:

1. How does the documentation of children's learning at Mangere Bridge Kindergarten, with *Te Whāriki* in mind, also reflect the children's preparation for school, with key competencies in mind?
2. In what ways did the curriculum-in-action at Mangere Bridge Kindergarten during the period of the Centre of Innovation provide opportunities, or an "affordance network", for the teaching and learning of key competencies?

The data for this chapter comes from Cree's 'kindergarten book', which is typical of the portfolios for the Mangere Bridge Kindergarten children. We chose this portfolio because when we were planning the writing of the final report, she was the most recent child to go to school and therefore had a complete portfolio for analysis. A Mangere Bridge Kindergarten portfolio includes the following range of artifacts, each of which has a different purpose:

> (i) personalised group Learning Stories, where Cree took part in an event or activity and the details of her participation are recorded
> (ii) individualised Learning Stories which are primarily about Cree's learning experience, although they often included other children.
> (iii) photographs of Cree's work
> (iv) celebrations at the kindergarten; these included farewells to children who were leaving, farewells to staff who were leaving, a valedictory and the story of the funeral of a beloved guinea pig, special events like 'Mat time in the new room', and a Special Persons evening when Cree's parents and two older sisters came to kindergarten and a photo was taken
> (v) excursions and visits in which Cree participated; ; her participation is not mentioned in the text but she might be included in a photograph
> (vi) group learning stories where Cree took part with a group in an event or an activity at the kindergarten, but the details of her participation are not recorded
> (vii) contributions from the family.

For the first of the two questions we analysed the entries under categories (i), (ii) and (iii). For the second question we included a survey of (iv), (v), (vi) and (vii) as well; the portfolio artifacts in these categories strengthened an "affordance network" (Barab & Roth, 2006; Gee, 2008; Wenger, 1998), to do with relationships and belonging to the kindergarten community, clearly a feature of the key competency *participation and contribution*. James Wertsch (1991) has argued that learners are not persons alone: they should be considered as "person(s)-with-mediational-means". Mediational means are resources, modes of communication and representation, and people, and they *afford* and are part of the learning. Contributions from the family when they revisited the portfolio at home or at kindergarten combined both purposes implicit in the two research questions for this chapter: contributing to a sense of belonging by connecting home and kindergarten, and contributing to our sense of Cree's learning by adding an interpretation from home.

Cree began kindergarten in the afternoon session (three afternoons a week) at age 3 years 6 months, in August of the first year of the transition project. She began the morning programme (five mornings a week) in April of the following year, at age 4 years 2 months, and began school the next year, just after her fifth birthday. The analysis here cannot do justice to the holistic nature of the portfolio for the reader: the range of artifacts, the lively texts of the stories, the diversity of format design using an extensive range of publishing software, and the quality of the photographs provided Cree and her family—and the research associates—with a vivid picture of Cree's developing identity as a learner. Her portfolio contained 60 entries, and their distribution across the major categories of portfolio artifacts is as follows: (i): 5; (ii): 27; (iii): 3; (iv): 10; (v): 6; (vi): 5; and (vii): 4.

We used the text in the school curriculum to assist us in the noticing, recognising and recording of Cree's key competency learning and the affordance network, and as we read Cree's stories we began to focus on a few aspects in order to deepen the story. Usually a story was coded with more than one of the five key competencies. Referring to a website, for instance, which Cree and the teachers (and Cree's family) did on several occasions in order to gain new information, was coded as *using language, symbols and texts* (using ICT), *participating* in communities beyond the local (a community of scientists, for instance, who are knowledgeable about sea shells), and *thinking* (being curious and asking questions). In the following discussion we have combined both of the research questions. The key competencies and the opportunities to learn them are closely interwoven, and this account of Cree's learning (using the key competency lens) is also an account of the teachers' teaching. Each of the five key competency headings is followed, in italics, by an excerpt from the annotation on pages 12 to 13 in the (New Zealand Curriculum) school curriculum document.

Key competency one: *thinking (exploration)*
intellectual curiosity, problem-solvers actively seek knowledge ... [and] ask questions

Cree's learning

In August of the second year that Cree was attending kindergarten, the portfolio recorded that "Cree arrived at kindergarten today with a question":

> "What sort of animals live in these shells?" I (Pat) wasn't quite sure, so Cree and I looked at some of the books on sea creatures, and found that one of her shells was a periwinkle. We couldn't find any information on the other shell, so we decided to look it up on the internet. After some searching we found a website that had pictures to identify shells. This was great! We worked our way down the list and Cree held her shell up close to the computer screen to compare it to the picture. Finally we found one shell that looked exactly like the one Cree had. The information only identified it by its scientific name, Turitella specie. We might need to keep looking to find a more common name for that shell, Cree. We also found out that both types of shell have a creature similar to a slug that lives inside them, and they use the hard covering of the shell for protection. Periwinkles mostly eat algae, and when they are young are often eaten by crabs. We wrote down the names of the shells and the website for Cree to take home. Your curiosity and questioning meant that we both learned something new today, Cree. Thankyou!

Photos were added, and also the website address. A parent added a note by hand to this story: "We have had some fun at home looking at this website too!" Earlier stories appear to be linked to this episode. In May that year the kindergarten children had been to a production by a Wellington theatre company entitled *Songs of the Sea*, and Cree had said that the best part was when Sean had "snatched the conch". In May Cree found a shell at the kindergarten and, copying another child, "listened" to its story (see below, under *using language, symbols and texts*). Other Stories add scientific information to Cree's portfolio or include an internet search. In a later story, in December of the second year, another kindergarten group joined the Mangere Bridge Kindergarten children to climb the local mountain (Mangere), and the story of how people came to this mountain (a journey by Hape from Hawaiiki) was included in all the children's portfolios. In February of her last year, Cree asked "Where were the pigeons?" after an excursion to a local landmark called Pigeon Mountain. Once again, the teacher, Cree and another child searched the internet for information. The Learning Story includes Cree's working theory that "Maybe Māori used to gather at Pigeon Mountain to hunt kereru [Māori pigeon]". Cree drew a picture of Pigeon Mountain and they sent a fax to the kindergarten near Pigeon Mountain, asking if they could help to answer the question. After Cree had left for school, one of the teachers found a book about Pigeon Mountain, and the teachers added a final comment to her portfolio:

> Cree said "We went to Pigeon Mountain, but there were no pigeons!" And then she wondered "How did Pigeon Mountain get its name?" ... You had

wondered whether it was because pigeons used to live there. Well, you were right. Also, lots of pigeon trees used to grow there too, and some people thought that might be why it was called Pigeon Mountain. Thank you for asking such an interesting question, Cree!

Opportunity to learn and develop this key competency

The affordance network that encouraged the development of this key competency included:

- the modelling by teachers of being curious and enjoying finding evidence and information
- the positioning of Cree as a thinker who asks interesting questions; these questions are taken seriously and there are resources for collaboratively seeking answers and working theories
- teachers who admitted that they were uncertain, encouraging co-constructed searches for answers
- the participation of the family and the opportunity to be curious about the 'real world' of shells and mountains outside the kindergarten walls.

The teachers had positioned Cree as someone who is curious, asks good questions, and helps others to pursue the answers. They also made it quite clear that that they didn't know the answers, and that they and the children were exploring together. Responding to Cree's first question ("What sort of animals live in these shells"), they sought information about shells from the community of knowledgeable scientists. Responding to the later question ("Where were the pigeons?"), they sought information from knowledgeable historians and geographers. So the quest for information connected with the community aspect of *participating and contributing*. The teachers were genuinely curious themselves.

Key competency two: *using language, symbols and texts (communication)*

using languages and symbols [as] systems for representing and communicating information, experience and ideas ... to produce texts of all kinds ... in a range of contexts; [students make] choices of language symbol and text; they confidently use ICT ... to access ... information and communicate with others

Cree's learning

Cree's portfolio includes 18 stories that illustrate her growing competence and interest in the use of language, in writing, drawing, dance, drama and story. On her first day at kindergarten she completed a 'picture in the art area and wrote her name on it'. In November that year, she dictated a play about Dr Silli, drew intricate drawings of each of the characters then cut them out and performed the play for one of the teachers.

> **SILLI DOCTORS**
> **A play by Cree**
>
> Doctors: Silli, Killi, Chilli, Cheesy
> Patient: Illi
>
> The Play: The big kid called Illi went to the doctors because she had a sore arm and a leg. And a tummy ache and a ache head, and a sore ear. Illi saw all the doctors, they fixed her. Because her arm had blood on it Doctor Chilli put a plaster on it. Then she got a lollipop from Doctor Killi. Then Illi went to the park with her Dad and then they went home to have lunch.
> THE END

In December of that year a painting was included in the portfolio: a painting with strong brush strokes, somewhat reminiscent of Chinese calligraphy. In May and June of the following year, drawings of butterflies and an insect, boldly drawn, appear, and on one of these a small butterfly appears as a sign in the corner. No more drawings appear in the portfolio, although in November a story is included of Cree and another child absorbed in mixing paint, "sometimes for painting and sometimes for enjoyment". Increasingly complex drama and associated story-telling and construction are described in the section below on *relating to others*, although they could belong here as well. Two stories, in November (*Maybe Music?*) and December (*Snow Angels in the Sandpit*) of her last full year at kindergarten, are worth re-telling here.

> *Maybe Music?*
> *Cree and teacher looking through her book.* 'We looked at all the stories detailing her learning. I (Jemma) asked her if she felt there was anything else she would like to have included. "I'll have to have a think about it." After a few minutes (thinking) she replied "I have an idea. Maybe music?" After a discussion she said she would like a CD of her favourite songs from kindergarten. I suggested we make a list of her favourite songs. "But how can I do that when I don't know how to write the words, and I can't read them," she exclaimed. "I know," she quickly answered herself "Why don't I listen to the songs and then I can tell you which ones I like and then you can write it down." Great idea Cree, and that's just what we did.'

This story also combines key competencies: a capacity and an inclination for critical *thinking* (considering what was missing in her portfolio), calling on *language symbols and texts* (music) to represent her time at kindergarten, and suggesting a final collaborative project (*self-management*) that will now *contribute* to the whole kindergarten community. The December story is simply a page of photographs of eight children lying, star-shaped in the sandpit. They have moved their arms up and down to look like angel wings, and the photos take a birds-eye view of eight 'angels'. The commentary says: "Snow Angels in the sandpit!! Wow what a great idea! Every day you [the collective?] seem to come up with something new".

Opportunity to learn and develop this key competency

The affordance network that encouraged the development of this key competency included:

- a programme in which literacy, in the widest sense, is integrated throughout
- a tradition of listening and writing down dictated stories
- resources for drawing and painting, movie-making and computer-generated illustrated stories (written by the children, as well as Learning Stories written by the teachers) are available and their use is supported.

Cree's art work and writing have, on the whole, been integrated with her storytelling and her projects, and the kindergarten programme has, as many do, been characterised by an integration of modes: in Cree's case, drama, drawing, sign-writing, dress-ups and block construction (see the strong argument for a multi-modal approach to making meaning in Kress, 2003, and Jewitt, 2008). The New Zealand early childhood curriculum has as one of its principles *ngā hononga* (the parallel in English is responsive and reciprocal relationships with people, places, and things). It is what learners do, and the affordance network of mediational means at Mangere Bridge Kindergarten provides opportunities for children to learn that. Teachers and children were searching books and websites for information to answer Cree's questions.

Key competency three: *managing self (well-being)*
[students] establish personal goals, make plans, manage projects, and set high standards

Cree's learning

There were seven learning episodes recorded in the portfolio where Cree was making plans and managing projects. Early in her kindergarten journey a teacher commented in her portfolio that 'Cree had a really good idea' when she made hand puppets from paper bags, and, later that month, that she was an 'inspiration to lots of children' when she found cardboard 'hands' in the carpentry area and decided to make them into wings. Over the next year Cree began to strengthen this disposition to creatively improvise with materials and to invent projects by setting herself ambitious challenges. She was working with teachers and other children in social contexts, a process that Iram Siraj-Blatchford has highlighted as 'sustained shared thinking' (Siraj-Blatchford & Manni, 2008), of value for strengthening the understanding of all involved in the sharing. Cree's projects were becoming more challenging and more sustained over time. She returned to her interest in shells over several episodes, she built 'homes' over two months with other children (also an example of *relating to others*), and there are stories of her exploring complex ideas with blocks in July, November and December of her last full year at kindergarten. Furthermore, by the end of that year her projects combined all of the key competencies. The following is a summary, adapted from the portfolio entry, of one of the later projects, entitled *Cree's Project*, in which she made some toys for her older sister's play mouse (using a glue gun, and a website for ideas).

> Once again, Cree arrived at kindergarten with a project in mind. She made a wheel/tunnel (photo) and asked "What toys did she need to make for (her sister)'s play mouse?" She and the teacher found a website that shared information about looking after rats and mice. It had a section on toys. Cree made a square tunnel, a ladder (with the hot glue gun) and a container for a bed. Cree showed another child how to make a ladder with the hot glue "in case she wanted to do it another time".

Cree's mother added continuity when she commented on the before and after events:

> Cree and (sister) had talked about Cree making a mouse house, earlier that morning. So Cree had thought a lot about how she was going to go about it. She had made everything a play mouse could possibly need! with some help from her kindy teachers. She has since made a house for her fairy Tinkerbell as well.

This Learning Story includes features from all five of the key competencies, including *participating and contributing*. The project crossed the borders of two communities: it was inspired at home, accomplished at kindergarten, and then continued at home in a different context. On this occasion, a teacher analysed the learning, using a school key competencies lens, as follows, and her evaluation is backed up by the evidence in the story.

> Cree is showing that she is a learner who asks questions, explores, thinks, discusses and explains [*thinking*]. She knows that information can be gathered from a range of sources, including books and the internet [*using language symbols and texts*]. Cree takes responsibility for her own learning and is willing to give things a go, choosing materials, solving problems and making decisions to reach her desired goals [*managing self*]. Cree shows her ability to work alongside others, sharing her knowledge and skills, supporting and contributing to the learning of others [*relating to others*].

The other four *'managing self'* projects in the same year were: *Making a helicopter out of Duplo*, and describing the sequence of the process (July); *Making a kite* ("Do you know what my favourite thing is to do? Fly a kite", August); *Building with blocks* (November); and *More building* (December). The latter two stories include aspects of *language symbols and texts*, *thinking creatively*, and *relating to others*, since they are examples of Cree and two other children building architecturally with two different kinds of blocks. The first of these building stories begins with the teacher saying, "Ever since we got the new blocks, they have been a source of inspiration and creativity". Cree and two others 'showed great skill' in 'balancing pieces, creating pleasing structures that included a wide range of shapes and sizes'. The teacher comments on the children's cooperation in selecting and sharing pieces, sharing ideas and offering provocation for each other. In the second build Learning Story (*More building*), 12 days later, Cree and two others (one of them is the same as in the November story) did more building with the white letter blocks. K. and Cree were making climbing walls. A. was building a pyramid. Cree explains the construction to the teacher ("When you have climbed to the top of the wall, that is the block you stand on").

Opportunity to learn and develop this key competency

The affordance network that encouraged the development of this key competency included:
- the time and opportunity to devise and carry out project plans
- responses to the children's ideas
- a range of open-ended resources that provide flexible affordances
- a culture in which the children improvised with resources that were not originally especially open-ended, enabling them to complete imaginative projects.

The programme provided many opportunities for the children to be resourceful problem-solvers, responding to the goals they set for themselves, and provoking them with new resources (e.g. the cardboard 'hands' in the carpentry area, the diversity of interesting websites, different kinds of blocks—Duplo, the Cities of the World blocks, and the white letter blocks), and support for their construction activities. At Mangere Bridge Kindergarten, teachers were on hand to listen to plans and purposes and to provide assistance. They had already established (see above, in the *thinking* examples) that they do not have all the answers, setting up a culture of collaborative problem-solving. The children retain the authorship of their plans and projects, and these projects therefore make sense to them (the making of toys for a 'play mouse' might not have the same imperative for an adult). The children, not the teachers, are also accountable for any of the project's shortcomings and failures. This positioning of children with authority is, according to James Greeno, crucial to the transfer of learning from one place and one context to another:

> I conjecture that authoritative and accountable positioning characterizes aspects of learning processes that are crucial for understanding transfer. The reason is that transfer, except in the simplest of cases, is an inherently authoritative action. By definition, transfer involves doing something that one has not been taught explicitly to do. (Greeno, 2006, p. 538)

Key competency four: *relating to others (contribution)*
interacting effectively with a diverse range of people in a variety of contexts; [it includes] the ability to recognise different points of view, negotiate, and share ideas

Cree's learning

Over the time she was attending kindergarten, Cree appeared to be increasingly able and more inclined to work and play with other children, negotiating and sharing ideas. In her first year she had developed the play cast and a script about Dr Silli and other characters (see *using language symbols and texts*) on her own, drawing the characters and performing the play for the teacher. Before that, she had invented ideas (puppets from paper bags, kite wings from cardboard hands) that other children copied. She had joined two other children in a role play that the teachers entitled '*The Shop*'. Cree explained to the teacher:

> "We are working in a shop and we are selling chips, strawberries, yoghurt, sugar, orange juice, straws and we also sell goodies". [Another child] added "Signs too. I am making signs to sell like 'stay away' and stuff". Cree sells some 'strawberries' and 'yoghurt' to the teacher.

In an analysis of the learning in *The Shop*, the teacher comments on the literacy, the team work and the collaboration. By mid-May and early June in the following year the plot-lines have become more complex and there are more children involved. In the May episode Cree appears to have a minor role (the cat). The following is a summary:

> *Our Home.* A group of girls built a 'home' for themselves on the climbing platform. Signs were 'written' and placed in prominent places: "No toys in our house because it's too full". "Don't come in the gate because the cats will think you're bad and attack you with their swords". "No naughty boys allowed, or naughty girls. We don't want you to get us ignored or hurt our baby". Cree was a cat.

The teacher adds:

> Perhaps this play was stimulated by our dramatic play at mat time. This involved story-telling using puppets and the masks we had made.

In an early June example, *More homes*, the story is more imaginative and challenging. Cree begins as 'the Dad Cat' and later became 'Ice Princess'. Drawing on the movies they have seen, five children weave a story-line and the teacher makes an attempt to write it down (the narrative as written does not appear to include Dad Cat or the Ice Princess):

> The family lived in their house until the baddies came along. Mr Invisible (who lived in the tree beside the house) is supposed to protect the family. He has invisible powers that help the family. He has electric in him. But when we are angry our hair flames up and then Shark Boy makes it straight again.

Opportunity to learn and develop this key competency

The affordance network that encouraged the development of this key competency included a culture of story-telling and movie-making, and an admiration for all dramatic enterprises. A number of the children's portfolios describe the movies that the children have planned, scripted, cast, costumed and filmed. Cree did not aim for these dizzy heights of collaborative endeavour, but all dramatic enterprises were valued and actively supported. At the same time, teachers note the occasions when children learned by watching and copying others—recognising the opportunities for children to learn from each other in projects, such as the collaborative block constructions in the previous section.

They provided and made costumes designed by the children, and were ready to assist with the construction of props. A 'What Next?' section in the *More homes* learning story suggests:

> [We, the teachers, could] provide a variety of materials such as the large blue netting (great for creating huts/homes), large cushions, tea sets, pots, stove, phones, computer keyboards, clip boards, old blankets, planks, ladders, more wooden boxes or reels, cardboard boxes etc.

Key competency five: participating and contributing

being actively involved in communities [that include] family, whānau and school and those based, for example, on a common interest or culture; they may be drawn together for purposes such as learning, work, celebration, or recreation; they may be local, national, or global; students who participate in communities have a sense of belonging and the confidence to participate within new contexts

Cree's learning

We have already described Cree's use of websites for finding information from, and therefore connecting with, science communities outside the kindergarten. Two entries in Cree's portfolios provide an account of school visits and include photos of Cree participating in school activities. A key co-participating community the portfolio includes is the family. There were nine entries from the family, hand-written at the end of a story (except for a photograph of puppies, e-mailed from home):

- an information sheet filled in by the family before Cree began
- a comment about her excitement and her comments before she began, added to a 'First day at kindergarten' (with photos) story
- a comment added to a story entitled *Sharing*, when her father called in at kindergarten and read her portfolio with her
- a comment about sharing the portfolio at home (including, "She had lots to tell me about at home. Cree likes to look at the photos of her friends who are now at school, and tells me she misses them")
- "Cree's vocabulary is certainly expanding" after a story in which Cree describes a helicopter she has built
- a comment about how the family had now referred to the website for information too
- "I heard the story about 'Grandma let me drive', it sounded very funny, Cree relayed the entire story to me", added after a story about a visit from the local librarian
- an explanation of the background information about the mouse house and mouse toys constructions
- a photo of puppies, added to the portfolio by the family.

'The day that Dad called in' also included a *relating to others* feature, because Cree noticed that James was hovering on the edge of this event, and she invited him to join in on the visit. Dad is mentioned again when one of the teachers discovered that she shared a birthday with him. The family spontaneously contributed a written comment to the portfolio on five occasions. Twice they personalised a group event by recounting Cree's comments about it at home. On one occasion, on a story that included Cree's conversation with the teacher, they made a comment about how her vocabulary was developing.

Opportunity to learn and develop this key competency

The affordance network that encouraged the development of this key competency included:

- the opportunities that the children's portfolios have provided for families to contribute to the assessment record
- a kindergarten that celebrates community events, and special occasions: artifacts in the portfolio (Learning Stories, photos, examples of work) in the categories (iv), (v), (vi) and (vii) are an aspect of assessment design that adds to the documentation of a kindergarten community of practice by including special events, celebrations, farewells, birthdays, excursions, and group events. Fifth birthday stories for other children, where Cree was invited by the 5-year-old to 'hold the birthday card' (a prized position), were included in her portfolio.
- portfolios that ensure that the interweaving of learning at the kindergarten and at home is 'reified'. 'Reification' is used in tandem with 'participation' by Etienne Wenger in his book on *Communities of Practice* (1998 pp. 57-71); it includes making participation and relationships 'concrete' or public in documents, and assessment formats that can be re-read or re-visited in other communities and at other times.

Concluding comments

This chapter has described the early childhood education and learning of one child at Mangere Bridge Kindergarten. Cree's portfolio is similar to all the portfolios of the children who are about to 'cross the bridge' into school; these portfolios provide a broad account of progress towards the vision in the New Zealand (school) Curriculum (p.7) of learners as 'Young people who will be confident, connected, actively involved, lifelong learners'. Cree is an example of a Mangere Bridge Kindergarten graduate as a *very* young person who is already a confident, connected, actively involved learner. The opportunities to learn have been part of this alignment. Teachers, families and other children have not been specifically working on something called 'preparation for school', but it is clear from the analysis of the teaching and learning, as presented in this kindergarten portfolio, that at the same time educational bridges are being built so that Cree will be ready willing and able to take this learning power forward as a lifelong learner. Many of the qualities described by the alignment between the strands of outcome in *Te Whāriki* and the key competencies in the school curriculum are seen in action here; they are also across-contexts-bridge-builders: being curious across a range of people places and things; understanding how to find knowledge when you don't know something that you want to know; resourceful problem-solving is encouraged and expected; ideas and stories are expressed and represented across a range of modes, and the learning is already travelling across the 'borders' to the family and the 'outside' world and back to the kindergarten.

CHAPTER 10

Conclusion

This transition to school project, based at Mangere Bridge Kindergarten, explored border crossing in terms of a community of children, families and teachers negotiating the transition from early childhood education to primary school. In New Zealand, in 2002 an early childhood strategic plan had recommended that both early childhood and school teachers should have an understanding of pedagogy and curriculum in the other sector (Ministry of Education, 2002). In 2007 a new school curriculum described an alignment between the strands of the early childhood curriculum and the key competencies at school (Ministry of Education, 2007). Enhancing transitions featured in other strategies and plans that followed (e.g., Ministry of Education, 2008a, 2008b). However, these policy documents only set the scene for transitions. As Peters (2008) has discussed, the alignment between the early childhood curriculum and the 2007 school curriculum provides a potential bridge to support children's learning across sectors, but the strength of the bridge depends on the connections that are deliberately made by both early childhood and school teachers. This is illustrated in Figure 5.

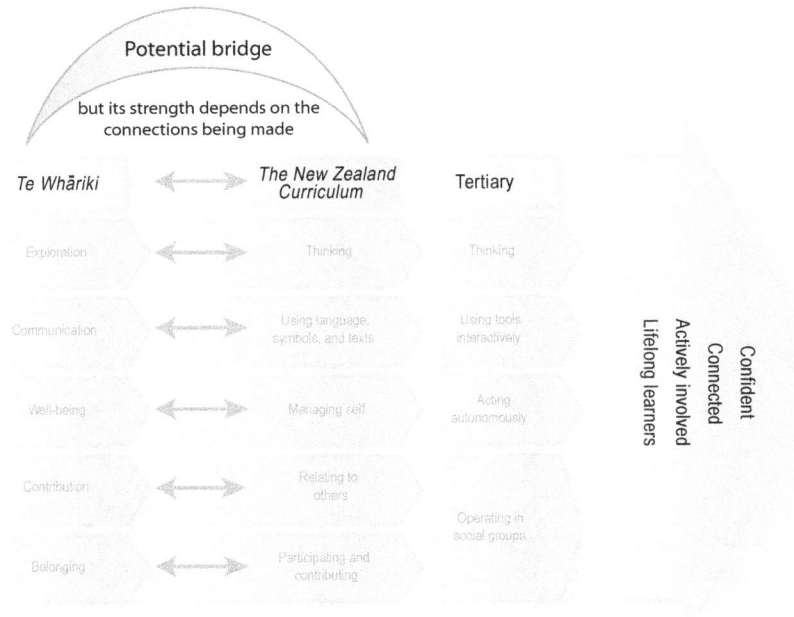

FIGURE 5: THE NEW CURRICULUM PROVIDES A POTENTIAL BRIDGE BETWEEN SECTORS

Source: Peters, 2008; adapted from Ministry of Education, 2007

This book has discussed some of the insights the Mangere Bridge project provided into the nature of these connections and how they can be strengthened. From the analysis of data, three key factors have been highlighted:
- good will and professional relationships between teachers in action
- fostering belonging and engagement in the new place
- recognising the continuity of learning journeys.

We will now look at each of these in turn.

Good will and professional relationships between teachers in action

Earlier studies had shown that good will alone is not sufficient to develop effective transition relationships (Robinson et al., 2000; Timperley et al., 2003). Actions are needed too. Where good will and interest exist, this study found that joint projects that were mutually interesting were a valuable way of fostering relationships—not just between teachers, but also between other members of the school and ECE communities. As was discussed in Chapter 7, the projects can be analysed by considering who initiates a project, the number of interested groups that are drawn in, and the strength of the mutual involvement. All the tasks offered some benefits, but the ones we found to be most effective in fostering relationships were those that had strong mutual interest from a range of participants.

The data illustrated that effective, professional relationships between early childhood settings and school teachers involved mutual respect and a balance of power. These relationships take time and persistence to develop, and have to be renegotiated as the staff changes and as projects develop. Flexibility, commitment and a 'can do' attitude were found to be important, and there are often stumbling blocks along the way. However, the positive benefits for all the transition participants (children, teachers and families) have indicated the value of developing these connections.

Fostering belonging and engagement in the new place

The bridge between sectors was strengthened by the many artifacts and activities that fostered both children's and their families' sense of belonging in the school context. The DVDs, visits, pamphlets, books and school display boards discussed in Chapter 4 were all examples of ways in which children and families can gain information about school and develop familiarity with the new setting, and hence gain confidence. Chapter 3 analysed the ways in which portfolios can empower children, enhance their identity as a learner, and provide a rich resource for connecting the funds of knowledge from home and the early childhood centre with the new learning at school. These were empowering for school teachers, too, as they provided insights into each child's funds of knowledge (Gonzales et al., 2005), which many teachers commented would take a lot longer to develop without this resource. As Learning Stories were added by the class teacher to the portfolios during children's visits to school, and later discussed at kindergarten, they provided insights about school for younger children when they read them in their friends' portfolios. Chapter 5 considered how strategies to support familiarity with the language, routines and practices of school assisted children's confidence and engagement in the new environment. Greater familiarity with the other setting assisted teachers and families as well. Chapter 6 described the ways in which learning about school and gaining confidence and competence could be enhanced further through engagement with older children in the buddies programme.

Recognising the continuity of learning journeys

In the Mangere Bridge community the kindergarten provided rich opportunities to learn. Aspects of this have been explored through Chapter 8, which considered the dynamic integrated multi-literacies that children were engaged in, and Chapter 9, which analysed the key competencies evident in the documentation in a kindergarten child's portfolio. These practices are not only valuable in their own right, but also act as priming events (Corsaro & Molinari, 2005) for the transition to school. Sensitive new entrant teachers picked up and built on these competencies, and some portfolios recorded this continuity, in a sense acting as 'passports' that could support the child's identity as a learner across contexts.

The research described in this book has provided valuable insights into both the ways in which transition experiences can be supported and the complexity of transition experiences. For example, strategies that initially appeared straightforward, such as taking the portfolios to school, revealed other issues to consider as the research cycles explored the strategies more deeply. As other communities draw on insights from the ideas discussed in this book, it will be important to remember that there are no simple recipes. Transitions are dynamic, multi-faceted (Ghaye & Pascal, 1988) and complex. The notion of 'effective transition practices', as described in the 10-year strategic plan, must be constantly revisited and evaluated within local contexts, taking into account the views of the many participants in the process.

REFERENCES

Aubrey, C., David, T., Godfrey, R., & Thompson, L. (2000). *Early childhood educational research: Issues in methodology and ethics*. London, UK: RoutledgeFarmer.

Barab, S. A., & Roth, W-M. (2006). Curriculum-based ecosystems: Supporting knowing from an ecological perspective. *Educational Researcher, 35*(5), 3-13. Available from www.jstor.org.ezproxy.waikato.ac.nz/stable/3699782.

Bell, J. (1999). *Doing your research project: A guide for first time researchers in education and social science*. Buckingham, UK: Open University Press.

Bird, L., & Drewery, W. (2000). *Human development in Aotearoa: A journey through life*. Manukau, NZ: McGraw-Hill.

Britt, C., & Sumsion, J. (2003). Within the borderlands: Beginning early childhood teachers in primary schools. *Contemporary Issues in Early Childhood, 4*(2), 115-136. Available from http://www.wwwords.co.uk.ezproxy.waikato.ac.nz/ciec/content/pdfs/4/issue4_2.asp#1.

Bronfenbrenner, U. (1979). *The ecology of human development: Experiments by nature and design*. Cambridge, MA: Harvard University Press.

Bronfenbrenner, U. (1986). Ecology of the family as a context for human development: Research perspectives. *Developmental Psychology, 22*(6), 723-742. Available from http://search.proquest.com.ezproxy.waikato.ac.nz/docview/614335518/1357A20AA7736CC143E/1?accountid=17287

Brooker, L. (2008). *Supporting transitions in the early years*. Berkshire, UK: McGraw-Hill.

Brostrom, S. (2002). Communication and continuity in the transition from kindergarten to school. In H. Fabian & A-W. Dunlop (Eds.), *Transitions in the early years: Debating continuity and progression for children in early education*. London, UK: RoutledgeFalmer.

Brostrom, S. (2005). Transition problems and play as transitory activity. *Australian Journal of Early Childhood, 30*(3), 17-25.

Brostrom, S. (2007). Transitions in children's thinking. In A. Dunlop & H. Fabian (Eds.), *Informing transitions in the early years: Research, policy and practice* (pp.52-63). Berkshire, UK: Open University Press.

Bulkeley, J., & Fabian, H. (2006). Well-being and belonging during the early educational transitions. *International Journal of transitions in Childhood, 2*. Available from http://extranet.edfac.unimelb.edu.au/LED/tec/pdf/journal2_bulkeley%20and%20fabian.pdf

Cardno, C. (2003). *Action research: A developmental approach*. Wellington: NZCER Press.

Carr, M. (1998). Taking dispositions to school: Keynote address to seminar on transition to school, *Childrenz Issues, 2*(1), 21-24.

Carr, M. (2001). *Assessment in early childhood settings: Learning stories*. London, UK: Paul Chapman.

Carr, M. (2006). Learning dispositions and key competencies: A new curriculum continuity across the sector? *SET: Research Information for Teachers, 2*, 23-27.

Carr, M., Lee, W., & Jones, C. (2004, 2007, 2009). *Kei Tua o te Pae Assessment for learning: Early Childhood Exemplars*. Books 1-20. A resource prepared for the Ministry of Education. Wellington, NZ: Learning Media.

Carr, M., Peters, S., Davis, K., Bartlett, C., Bashford, N., Berry, P., et al (2008). *Key learning competencies across place and time: Kimihia te ara tōtika, hei oranga mō to aō*. Teaching Learning Research Initiative Final Report. Available from: http://www.tlri.org.nz/key-learning-competencies-across-place-and-time/

Cochran-Smith, M., & Donnell, K. (2006). Practitioner inquiry: Blurring the boundaries of research and practice. In J. L. Green, G. Camilli, P. B. Elmore, A. Skukauskaité, & P. Grace (Eds.), *Handbook of complementary methods in education research* (pp. 503-518). Washington, DC: AERA; & Mahwah, NJ: Erlbaum.

Commissioner for Children, (2006). Te Ara Tukutuku Nga Whanaungatanga o Nga Tamariki: Weaving pathways to wellbeing—an integrated framework for children and their families. *Children: A Newsletter from the Office of the Children's Commissioner*, Summer 2006, No. 59, 4-6.

Cosaro, W.A. (2005). *The sociology of childhood* (2nd ed.). Thousand Oaks, CA: Pine Forge Press.

Corsaro, W., & Molinari, L. (2005). *I Compagni: Understanding children's transitions from preschool to elementary school*. New York, NY: Teachers College Press.

Curtis, D., & Carter, M. (2003). *Designs for living and learning: Transforming early childhood environments*. St Paul: Redleaf Press.

Dockett, S., & Perry, B. (1999). Starting school: What matters for children, parents and educators? *AECA Research in Practice Series, 6*(3).

Dockett, S., & Perry, B. (2001). Starting school: Effective transitions. *Early Childhood Research & Practice, 3*(2). Available on-line http://ecrp.uiuc.edu/v3n2/dockett.html

Dockett, S., & Perry, B. (2002). Who's ready for what? Young children starting school. *Contemporary Issues in Early Childhood, 3*(1), 67-89. Available from http://www.wwwords.co.uk.ezproxy.waikato.ac.nz/ciec/content/pdfs/3/issue3_1.asp#4

Dockett, S., & Perry, B. (2003, September). *Children's voices in research on starting school*. Paper presented at the 13th annual conference of the Early Childhood Education Research Association, Glasgow.

Dockett, S., & Perry, B. (2005). "A buddy doesn't let kids get hurt in the playground: Starting school with buddies". *International Journal of Transitions in Childhood, 1*, 22-34.

Dockett, S., & Perry, B. (2007). *Transitions to school: Perceptions, expectations and experiences*. Sydney: University of New South Wales Press.

Early, D. M., Pianta, R. C., & Cox, M. J. (1999). Kindergarten teachers and classrooms: A transition context. *Early Education and Development, 10*(1), 25-46.

Ecclestone, K. (2009). Lost and found in transition: Educational implications of concerns about 'identity', 'agency' and 'structure'. In J. Field, J. Gallacher, & R. Ingram (Eds.), *Researching transitions in lifelong learning*. Oxon: Routledge.

Educational Transitions and Change (ETC) Research Group. (2011). *Transition to school: Position statement*. Albury-Wodonga: Research Institute for Professional Practice, Learning and Education, Charles Sturt University.

Einarsdottir, J. (2006). From pre-school to primary school: When different contexts meet. *Scandinavian Journal of Educational Research, 50*(2), 165-184.

Fabian, H. (1998). *Induction to school and transition through key stage one: Practice and perceptions*. Unpublished PhD thesis Coventry University.

REFERENCES

Fabian, H., & Dunlop, A. (Eds.). (2002). *Transitions in the early years: Debating continuity and progression for young children in education.* London, UK: RoutledgeFalmer.

Fasoli, L. (2003). Reflections on doing research with children. *Australian Journal of Early Childhood, 28*(1), 7-12.

Fleer, M. (2002). Sociocultural assessment in early years education – myth or reality. *International Journal of Early Years Education, 10*(2), 105-120.

Gee, J. P. (2008). A sociocultural perspective on opportunity to learn. In P. A. Moss, D. C. Pullin, J. P. Gee, E. H. Haertel, & L. J. Jones Young (Eds.), *Assessment, equity, and opportunity to learn.* (pp.76-108). New York, NY: Cambridge University Press.

Ghaye, A., & Pascal, C. (1988). Four-year-old children in reception classrooms: Participant perceptions and practice. *Educational Studies, 14*(2), 187-208.

Gipps, C. (1999). Socio-Cultural aspects of assessment. *Review of Research in Education, 24,* 355-392.

Giroux, H. (1992). *Border crossings: Cultural workers and the politics of education.* New York, NY: Routledge.

Gonzales, N., Moll, L. C., & Amanti, C. (2005). *Funds of knowledge: Theorizing practices in households, communities and classrooms.* Mahwah, NJ: Erlbaum.

Graue, E., & Walsh, D. (1998). *Studying children in context: Theories, methods and ethics.* London, UK: Sage Publications.

Greeno, J.G. (2006). Authoritative, accountable positioning and connected, general knowing: Progressive themes in understanding transfer. *Journal of the Learning Sciences, 15*(4), 537-547.

Hamre, B. K., & Pianta, R. C. (2007). Learning opportunities in preschool and early elementary classrooms. In R. Pianta, M. Cox, & K. Snow (Eds.), *School readiness & the transition to kindergarten in the era of accountability.* Baltimore: Paul Brookes.

Healy, A. (2008). *Multiliteracies and diversity in education: New pedagogies for expanding landscapes.* Melbourne, Vic: Oxford University Press.

Hill, S., Comber, B., Louden, W., Rivalland, J. (1998). *100 children go to school: Connections and disconnections in literacy development in the year prior to school and the first year of school.* Canberra, ACT: Department of Employment, Education, Training and Youth Affairs.

Jewitt, C. (2008). Multimodality and literacy in school classrooms. In G. J. Kelly, A. Luke, & J. Green (Eds.), *Review of research in education: What counts as knowledge in educational settings, 32*(7), 241-267.

Kagan, S. L., & Lowenstein, A. E. (2004). School readiness and childrens play: Contemporary oxymoron or compatible option? In E. Zigler, D. Singer, & S. Bishop-Josef (Eds.), *Children's play: The roots of reading.* (pp. 33-49). Washington: Zero to Three Press.

Kagan, S., & Neuman, M. (1998). Lessons from three decades of transition research. *Elementary School Journal, 98*(4), 365-380.

Kamler, B., & Comber, B. (2005). Designing turn-around pedagogies and contesting deficit assumptions. In B. Comber & B. Kamler (Eds.), *Turn-around pedagogies: Literacy interventions for at risk students.* Newtown, NSW: Primary English Association.

Kemmis, S., & McTaggart, R. (2000). Participatory action research. In N. K. Denzin, & Y. S. Lincoln (Eds.), *Handbook of qualitative research* (2nd ed.) (pp. 567-605). London: Sage

Kress, G. (2003) *Literacy in the new media age.* London, UK: Routledge.

Lankshear, C., & Knobel, M. (2003). *New literacies: Changing knowledge and classroom learning.* Buckingham, UK: Open University Press.

Ledger, E. (2000). *Children's perspectives of their everyday lives with a focus on the transition from early childhood center to school.* Unpublished PhD thesis University of Otago, Dunedin.

Lenz Taguchi, H. L. (2006). Reconceptualising early childhood education: Challenging taken-for-granted ideas. In J. Einarsdottir & J. Wagner (Eds.), *Nordic childhoods and early education.* Greenwich, MA: Information Age Publishing.

Makin, L., Jones Diaz, C., & McLachlan, C. (2007). *Literacies in childhood: Changing views, challenging practice.* Marrickville, NSW: Elsevier.

Mapa, L., Sauvao, L., & Podmore, V. (2000, December). *Transition to school from Pacific Islands early childhood services: Research processes and main findings.* Paper presented at the annual conference of the New Zealand Association for Research in Education, Hamilton.

Margetts, K. (2002). Planning transition programmes. In H. Fabian, & A-W. Dunlop (Eds.), *Transitions in the early years: Debating continuity and progression for children in early education.* London, UK: RoutledgeFalmer.

Margetts, K. (2007). Understanding and supporting children: Shaping transition practices. In A. Dunlop & H. Fabain (Eds.), *Informing transitions in the early years: Research, policy and practice* (pp. 111-122). Berkshire, UK: Open University Press.

McFarlane, A., Glynn, T., Grace, W., Penetito, W., & Bateman, S. (2008). Indigenous epistemology in a national curriculum framework. *Ethnicities 8*, 102-127.

McNaughton, S. (2001). Co-constructing expertise: The development of parents and teachers ideas about literacy practices and the transition to school. *Journal of Early Childhood Literacy, 1*(1), 40-58.

Mills, G. (2000). *Action research: A guide for the teacher researcher.* NJ: Prentice Hall.

Ministry of Education. (1993). *The New Zealand Curriculum Framework.* Wellington: Learning Media.

Ministry of Education. (1996). *Te whāriki. He whāriki mātauranga mō ngā mokopuna o Aotearoa: Early childhood curriculum.* Wellington: Learning Media.

Ministry of Education. (2002). *Pathways to the future: Nga huarahi arataki: A 10 year strategic plan for Early Childhood Education.* Wellington: Learning Media.

Ministry of Education. (2007). *The New Zealand curriculum.* Wellington: Learning Media.

Ministry of Education. (2008a). *Ka hikitia—managing for success: The Māori education strategy 2008-2012.* Retrieved 16 March 2009, from www.educationcounts.govt.nz.

Ministry of Education. (2008b). *Pasifika education plan 2008-2012.* Wellington: Ministry of Education.

Ministry of Health. (2008). *B4 school check.* Available from http://www.moh.govt.nz/b4schoolcheck

Mutch, C. (2005). *Doing educational research: A practitioners guide to getting started.* Wellington: NZCER Press.

New London Group. (2000). A pedagogy of multiliteracies. In B. Cope & M. Kalantzis, (Eds.), *Multiliteracies: Literacy learning and design of social futures* (pp. 9 -37). South Yarra, Vic: MacMillan.

Nicholson, T. (2005). *At the cutting edge: The importance of phonemic awareness in learning to read and spell.* Wellington: NZCER Press.

Nutbrown, C., & Clough, P. (2009). Citizenship and inclusion in the early years: Understanding and responding to children's perspectives on 'belonging'. *International Journal of Early Years Education, 17*(3), 191-206.

Paley, V. G. (2004). *A child's play: The importance of fantasy play.* Chicago, IL: University of Chicago Press.

REFERENCES

Pere, R. (1982). *Ako: Concepts and learning in the Maori tradition.* Working paper No.17. Hamilton: Department of Sociology, University of Waikato.

Peters, S. (2002). *Talking about transition: exploring different perspectives in order to foster a collaborative approach.* Keynote address at Te Riu Roa Conference. Wellington: New Zealand.

Peters, S. (2003). "I didn't expect that I would get tons of friends… more each day": Children's experiences of friendship during the transition to school. *Early Years: Journal of International Research and Development, 23,* 45-53.

Peters, S. (2004). *Crossing the border: An interpretive study of children making the transition to school.* Unpublished PhD thesis University of Waikato.

Peters, S. (2008, September). *Learning dispositions to key competencies: Navigating learning journeys across the border from early childhood education to school.* Paper presented to Images of Transition at the European Early Childhood Education Research Association 18th annual conference, Stavanger University, Norway.

Peters, S. (2010). Literature review: Transition from early childhood education to school. Report commissioned by the Ministry of Education. Wellington: Ministry of Education. Available from: http://www.educationcounts.govt.nz/publications/ece/78823

Peters, S., Hartley, C., Rogers, P., Smith, J., & Carr, M. (2009). Early childhood portfolios as a tool for enhancing learning during the transition to school. *International Journal of Transitions in Childhood. 3,* 4-15. Available at http://extranet.edfac.unimelb.edu.au/LED/tec/journal_vol3.shtml

Phillips, G., McNaughton, S., MacDonald, S., & Keith, M. (2002). *Picking up the pace.* Wellington: Ministry of Education.

Robinson, V., Timperley, H., & Bullard, T. (2000). *Strengthening education in Mangere and Otara evaluation: Second evaluation report.* Auckland: The University of Auckland.

Rogoff, B. (1990). *Apprenticeship in thinking: Cognitive development in social context.* New York, NY: Oxford University Press.

Rychen, D. S., & Salganik L. S. (2001). (Eds.). *Defining and selecting key competencies.* Göttingen, Germany: Hogrefe & Huber.

Rychen, D. S., & Salganik L. S. (2003). *Key competencies for a successful life and a well-functioning society.* Göttingen, Germany: Hogrefe & Huber.

Saracho, O., & Spodek, B. (2003). Recent trends and innovations in the early childhood education curriculum. *Early Child Development and Care, 173*(2), 175-183.

Segal, M. (2004). The roots and fruits of pretending. In E. Zigler, D. Singer, & S. Bishop-Josef (Eds.), *Children's play: The roots of reading.* (pp.33-49). Washington: Zero to Three Press.

Siraj-Blatchford, I., & Manni, L. (2008). Would you like to tidy up now? An analysis of adult questioning in the English Foundation Stage. *Early Years: International Journal of Research and Development 28*(1), 5-22.

Smith, A. (1998). *Understanding children's development: A New Zealand perspective.* Wellington: Bridget Williams Books.

Suggate, S. P. (2009). School entry age and reading achievement in the 2006: Programme for international student assessment (PISA). *International Journal of Educational Research 48,* 151–161.

Tangaere, A. R. (1998). Maori human development learning theory. In P. Te Whaiti, M. McCarthy, & A. Durie (Eds.), *Mai I rangiatea: Maori wellbeing and development.* Wellington: Auckland University Press/Bridget Williams Books.

Thomson, P. (2002). *Schooling the rustbelt kids: Making the difference in changing times.* Sydney: Allen & Unwin.

Thomson, P., & Hall, C. (2008). Opportunities missed and/or thwarted? 'Funds of knowledge' meet the english national curriculum. *Curriculum Journal, 19*(2), 87-103.

Timperley, H., McNaughton, S., Howie, L., & Robinson, V. (2003). Transitioning children from early childhood education to school: Teacher beliefs and transition practices. *Australian Journal of Early Childhood, 28*(2), 32-40.

Unsworth, L. (2001). Describing visual literacies. In L. Unsworth (Ed.), *Teaching multiliteracies across the curriculum* (pp. 71-112). Buckingham, UK: Open University Press.

Vygotsky, L. (1978). *Mind in society: The development of higher psychological processes.* Cambridge, MA: Harvard University Press.

Wenger, E. (1998). *Communities of practice: Learning, meaning and identity.* New York, NY: Cambridge University Press.

Wertsch, J. V. (1991). *Voices of the mind: A sociocultural approach to mediated action.* Cambridge, MA: Harvard University Press.

Wertsch, J. V., & Tulviste, P. (1992). L. S. Vygotsky and contemporary developmental psychology. *Developmental Psychology, 28*(4), 548-557.

www.ingramcontent.com/pod-product-compliance
Lightning Source LLC
Chambersburg PA
CBHW080637230426
43663CB00016B/2899